Take It
Back

Take It Back

THE PERSONAL POWER YOU GIVE AWAY EVERYDAY

Kay Potetz, Ph.D.

Foreword by
Dr. Mary Jen Meerdink, Psychologist

Crooked River Publishing Company
Lakewood, OH

© 2012 Kay Potetz

All rights reserved. No part of this publication may be reproduced, stored in retrieval system, or transmitted in any form or by any means electronic, mechanical, photocopying, recording or otherwise, without the prior written permission of the publisher.

Published by
Crooked River Publishing Company
Lakewood, OH

Publisher's Cataloging-in-Publication Data
Potetz, Kay.

   Take it back : the personal power you give away everyday / Kay Potetz. – 1st ed. - Lakewood, OH : Crooked River Pub., 2012.

   p. ; cm.

   ISBN13: 978-0-9860062-0-3

   1. Self-actualization (Psychology) 2. Emotional intelligence. 3. Attitude (Psychology) 4. Change (Psychology) 5. Interpersonal relations. I. Title.

BF637.S4 P67 2012
158.1—dc23   2012937557

FIRST EDITION

Project coordination by Jenkins Group, Inc.
www.BookPublishing.com

Cover and interior illustrations by Darren Cranford
Cover design by Chris Rhoads
Interior design by Yvonne Fetig Roehler

Printed in the United States of America
16 15 14 13 12 • 5 4 3 2 1

For my late parents
Madge Folger Potetz 1927–2002
Bill Potetz 1926–2001

and my three mentors in life:
1. Alfred Armstead 1929–2008
2. Betty Brooks 1925–1995
3. Carrie Stratis 1927–

With love and respect for all of you.
Thank you.

CONTENTS

    Foreword ix

    Acknowledgments xiii

1 What Is Personal Power? 1

2 I Never Saw It Coming 15

3 Assumptions, Attitudes, and Beliefs 23

4 The Pygmalion Effect: You Get What You Expect 35

5 Goodbye Excuses 47

6 Emotional Intelligence, Self-Awareness, and "Blind Spots" ... 61

7 What's My Part in This Drama? 79

8 Have You Ever Been Hijacked?—Emotionally, That Is 95

9 Actions and Reactions 109

10 Self-Respect 125

11 I'm Sorry, You're Sorry—Or Are We? 139

12 Leaving Behind the "They" Mentality 153

13 Get a Grip on Your Life 165

    Selected Bibliography 179

    Recommended Reading 183

    About the Author 185

FOREWORD

We live in a world in which so much feels beyond our individual control. Rapidly shifting work environments, economic tumult, changes in social norms and expectations, and the overall dizzying pace of life can leave us feeling like "passengers" rather than "drivers" of our own lives. Daily, we encounter many problematic situations that can seem like roadblocks on our intended road to progress.

Within this increasingly complex, challenging environment, our universal human longings persist. Most prominent are two: the desire to feel at ease with ourselves and our circumstances and the desire to feel in control over our own lives. In a nutshell, beneath all of our differences, we Homo sapiens just want to get through the day with a little less frustration and a little more pleasantness. And along the way, we want to feel we are "doers" rather than "the done to."

But our internal desires are in constant conflict with external forces—which can leave us feeling powerless. How can we attain consistent peace of mind when everything around us is running amok? In such an unpredictable environment, the idea of developing sustainable happiness and satisfaction in our lives seems truly radical. Furthermore, to achieve this while maintaining lightness and a sense of humor sounds downright impossible!

What this book offers is just that: a means of harnessing the power with which you were born to attain lasting, resilient happiness. No, it isn't a magic wand . . . well, not literally. But it does offer a highly practical pathway to an entirely new way of seeing the world, one that—as a result— leads to greater satisfaction and well-being at work, among loved ones, and even while watching the evening news. Integrating well-documented science with real-life examples that will make you wonder if she has been peeking in your windows, Dr. Potetz gives the reader a wealth of simple, user-friendly tools for living a happier life . . . strategies that require neither heavy-lifting nor military coups. In fact, you can make this transformation while managing to laugh . . . a lot!

Dr. Potetz shows us that personal power is an extremely valuable, readily accessible (and all too underutilized) resource. She distinguishes between "power over others" (often appearing in our world as manipulation and domination) and "power over ourselves" (choosing how to make meaning of all that transpires around us). Through research and anecdote, she reveals that perception is reality—our sense of well-being is far more a product of our beliefs and expectations than what is "actually" taking place in any given situation. She uncovers the hidden price of seeing oneself as a victim of external circumstances. She also shows us the many benefits of living by the truism that "What You Do Is What You Get," or WYDIWYG for short. The book addresses not only the psychological and emotional but also the physiological ways that our choices impact our experience of well-being.

As a Gestalt-oriented psychologist and coach, I often speak with clients about power. Specifically, a very simple equation exists: greater self-awareness offers us choices, and choices offer us power. Only by looking at ourselves honestly—and changing our habitual worldview—can we see alternatives. A greater repertoire of choices inherently implies greater personal power. If we insist on seeing our happiness as a product of who does or doesn't do this or that, and if we rely on an unconscious set of expectations, we remain painfully limited in our options. We become shackled by our own limiting beliefs. Powerless. Take it Back: Your Power, That Is offers fun but extremely substantive lessons for developing self-efficacy and satisfaction and freeing ourselves from the burden of things beyond our control.

As an organizational consultant, I routinely work with leaders who find themselves in restrictive organizational structures. Like most human beings—and all great leaders—they want to be as productive and happy as possible within the immediate constraints of the system. Obviously, I cannot (usually) promise them an instant, total overhaul of the structure of their companies. But I can help them recognize their own power: the power to reduce reactivity, negativity, and disengagement within themselves and those they lead. This book offers me (and all who share my mission of supporting personal and organizational effectiveness) a truly exciting and very accessible resource for all of my clients.

Dr. Potetz brings to this book the same highly engaging, matter-of-fact, humor-infused tone that routinely brings her standing ovations everywhere she speaks, both nationally and internationally. Without self-consciousness, she includes her own foibles as fair game in the conversation: this is a human condition, she wants us to know, and none of us are exempt. So we can all just relax, take ourselves a bit less seriously, and have some fun as we start to own more responsibility and bring greater satisfaction into every facet of our lives. Easy medicine to take!

If you read this book, I can guarantee you three things: First, it will repeatedly evoke smiles of self-recognition—you will feel like you're in on the joke. Second, you will recommend it to no fewer than three friends. And third, if you incorporate even a few of her ideas, you will feel significantly more satisfaction and peace in your daily life, no matter what is going on around you! So I encourage you to try it: Take back your power. With this book, the road to attaining your deepest desires is not only painless, but a lot of fun.

— Dr. Mary Jen Meerdink, Psychologist
Beachwood, OH & Evergreen, CO
www.Northstar4results.com

ACKNOWLEDGMENTS

- Linda Rich, my dear life friend, who's been with me for many years, providing friendship and much-needed encouragement in the process of writing of this book. Thank you for being there.
- Barb Folger Semple, a family member. You know who you are and what you've done over the years. Thank you.
- Virginia McCullough, my writing coach, without whom this book would not have been completed. I appreciate your expertise, candor, and patience. Thank you.
- Dr. Pauline Clance: Many years ago, you helped me get to know myself and build my confidence. Thank you for your professionalism, love, and friendship over the years.
- Betty Jo Armstead: You've been a friend for many years. You were there for all of the ups and downs in my life's journey. Thank you.
- Dr. Mary Jen Meerdink, my business associate for many years. Thank you for your input, coaching, friendship, and love.
- Fred DeGrandis, Cleveland Clinic Health System: Thank you for providing me the opportunity to lecture and present this material to

countless CCHS employees over the years. As they say, "Practice makes perfect." It's always a pleasure working with you.

- Laura Navin, CCHS, Medina Hospital, who assisted me in developing the concept and idea for my trademark, i.e., WYDIWYG.
- Mom, Dad, Betty, and Al, I wish you could have read this.

1

WHAT IS PERSONAL POWER?

> Life is 10% what happens to you and 90% how you react to it.
> — Charles Swindoll

Does this sound familiar? *I was in such a good mood when I walked into my office this morning. Everything was going great. I'd slept well, felt rested, and was ready to begin a new day—and then he arrived.*

The "he" of this story is the guy who comes into your office without an appointment, who makes unreasonable demands and acts nasty and rude. This morning was no different. Today he was on his usual crusade, loudly shouting, "You overcharged me!" And as usual, you hadn't overcharged him; he just didn't understand the billing system. But by the time he finally left, he had upset everyone within earshot and left you physically and mentally drained—and it was only 11:30 a.m. He had ruined your morning.

Because of him, the rest of your day was filled with irritations and annoyances. Supply deliveries were late, angry customers were complaining, and two coworkers called in sick—which meant you had to do triple the work. Heaven forbid that management hire another person to help. And on top of everything else, the copier broke down and the repair person couldn't come in to fix it until the end of the week. The whole week was messed up.

Or, how about this: Yesterday, Sam went out of his way to hold a door open for someone who breezed on through without thanking him. How rude! *"You're welcome,"* Sam muttered to himself through clenched teeth. He wished people had better manners—doesn't anyone care about being considerate anymore? He fell into a bad mood and thought that everybody was rude to him for the rest of the day.

Here's another situation: A friend asked Betty to come to a workshop to learn how to make jewelry. It sounded like fun, but Betty quickly refused the invitation. "I'm not good at crafts and arty things," she said. "I'm all thumbs, and I'm not that creative anyway." Betty's friend, although disappointed, accepted her answer and asked another friend to accompany her to the class. *It really doesn't matter,* Betty thought. Besides, Betty believed she didn't have time for that nonsense.

Marianne is still fuming over her last shopping trip. Getting to her car in the parking lot was a nightmare. She was all loaded up: bags hung from her arms while she struggled to carry a stack of boxes. Anybody with half a brain would notice that she needed assistance, wouldn't they? At least a dozen people looked right at her but didn't offer to help. Some people walked by and acted as if she wasn't even there. Whatever happened to "do unto others?" She went about her business that day feeling bitter and annoyed.

How many of your greetings have been ignored? You smile and say, "Good Morning," and reasonably expect the same in return. Instead you're ignored or maybe receive a nasty look. It affects your outlook so much that you need to tell everybody exactly what happened. You want anyone who will listen to know how terribly rude some folks are.

All drivers have experienced this. While driving home in traffic after a long day, we hear a horn blaring from another car. Before we know it, the driver of that car passes around us and then cuts in front of us, shouting and swearing. Our usual reaction is anger; many of us might immediately floor the accelerator, pull around his car, and try to cut him off—just to show him what it feels like. Who does he think he is?

Seemingly trivial, these unpleasant everyday events illustrate the small ways in which we give away our *personal power*. In these examples, we see ourselves reacting to and judging others, thinking about what should've been done or said. They behaved poorly! They were wrong! You wouldn't think of doing anything so rude, and if you did, somebody would nail you for sure.

JUDGMENT: THE GRAND ENERGY STEALER

Imagine how much energy we waste judging and reacting to other people's behavior. On any given day, we have many opportunities to observe, interpret, and judge the actions of others. (Do I hear you exclaiming, "What? Judge? I am *not* judgmental!")

Believe me, I understand that reaction. After all, aren't we all taught that judging another person is both improper and discourteous, and may even flirt with the edges of sin?

I remember my grandmother's words: "Like the Good Book says, Kay, 'Judge not, lest ye be judged.'"

When I talk about judgments, I'm not referring to being judgmental in the pejorative sense. You've probably experienced one of the above situations, but were unaware of the role that judgment played in the event. The word "judgmental" has a negative ring to it; most of us sincerely believe that we aren't judgmental and reject any suggestion that links us to this behavior. On the other hand, we praise people who we think have good judgment. I know. It's a bit confusing.

The fact is we're all judgmental. If we weren't, we'd all dress alike, drive identical cars, and live in matching houses and neighborhoods. And of course we don't. Therefore, each of us must make many judgments throughout the day: what time to get up, what to wear, where to eat, with whom we associate, and so on. Without actively judging things in our lives, we wouldn't get anywhere or finish anything. How could we? So does being judgmental help us? The answer is discomforting: both "yes" and "no."

Remember what your mother said: "It's not *what* you said; it's *how* you said it." Being judgmental is much like that. It's not *that* you judge, but rather *what* you judge. Getting through life requires us to make judgments, and if we stick with judging only that which is in our control—what to wear, where to go, or what we want to do—all is well. It's judging others that creates our stress: "*He* shouldn't do that," or "*She* should've said, 'thank you.'" Regardless of what you think is appropriate behavior for others, you have no control over what they say or do. This kind of misplaced judgment is a primary source of frustration and stress in our lives.

When we feel annoyed, we usually look for some kind of cause. If we can pinpoint "who started it," we can get rid of what's bugging us. You know what I mean: "If it weren't for you, I could've finished," or, "Because of you, we'll all be late," or the ever-popular, "Who started this?" But identifying the cause of a problem isn't always part of the solution. Once the "cause" is exposed, we might direct our anger toward the perceived perpetrator—and if he or she isn't available, we'll rant and rave at the first person we see. At the "end of our rope," we might bombard innocent bystanders with rage, nasty comments, and intimidation. Many of us refer to this as "venting." Once *they* know we're angry, the situation changes and we feel better. Right?

Sadly, this assumption couldn't be more incorrect. Anger and rage usually inflame an already bad situation—like throwing gasoline on an open fire. The only thing that changes is how you're perceived: "Boy, she's really unreasonable," or, "What a hothead," or, "Stay away from her; she flies off the handle easily."

While most of us are sincere in our problem-solving efforts, anger usually trumps any positive intention. The initial situation gets worse: we're upset and might do something offensive or harmful. If we apologize, we'll usually say something like: "I got so mad, I just couldn't help myself. I said things I didn't mean, and I'm sorry." However, the most severe damage comes at a personal, physical level—anger and rage prompt powerful physiological reactions in our body.

In his book *Emotional Intelligence*, Daniel Goleman posits that anger creates stress by increasing our heart rate and blood pressure. When episodes of anger are frequent, damage occurs as "the turbulence of blood flowing through the coronary artery with each heartbeat can cause microtears in the vessel where plaque develops." Other organs are harmed by anger and rage as well—i.e., the nervous, musculoskeletal, respiratory, endocrine, gastrointestinal, reproductive, and immune systems. I focus on the heart, because when it stops, we're finished.

Some of us believe that our anger is automatic and cannot be controlled. We've all heard things like: "*He* made me angry," or "*She* is the cause of my reaction." This seems real to many of us because, once we get angry, our feelings escalate and seem unstoppable. Goleman says, "Anger builds on anger; the emotional brain heats up. By then rage, unhampered by reason, quickly erupts into violence. At this point people are unforgiving and beyond being reasoned with; their thoughts revolve around revenge and reprisal." Whew! I get tired just talking about the energy it takes for all that.

The act of judgment is a source of personal power and is essential to succeed in life. Unfortunately, when misused, it can have disastrous results.

The next time you're irritated or annoyed, ask yourself: *Is this something I can control?* If not, let it go. If you don't, your irritation will grow—damaging your thoughts, ruining your plans, and spilling onto others. The Serenity Prayer asks for the ability to accept the things we cannot change, the courage to change the things we can, and the wisdom to know the difference.

Instead we spend much of our day reacting and responding to other people's behavior, comments, and actions (or inactions). Unless we're hermits in caves or on mountaintops, *we exchange emotions with others all day long*. We react physically to disappointments and unmet expectations from coworkers, from friends and family, and even from strangers. All this takes energy, and by the end of the day we might feel as if our "get-up-and-go" is gone. These unsatisfying interactions diminish us both physically and mentally. In essence, they're a loss of personal power: *the power you have to make decisions about what you will or will not do in life.* The ability to say no—and the capacity to set and maintain personal boundaries—requires the use of one's personal power. If we use it up on others, we have none left for ourselves.

This book is about personal power—the ways we give it away and how we retrieve it. I'm not referring to positional power *(I'm the boss, so you have to do what I say)* or referential power *(I'm the expert here, so I'll make the decisions).* I'm talking about personal power. This is the power each of us has and unknowingly gives away throughout the day.

Rather than examining the power we have over others, we'll focus on the personal power we have over ourselves—which, in reality, is the only thing we have the ability to control. An act of judgment usually results in a reaction to a person or situation. If it's something we like, our reaction is positive and we feel good. However, when we judge something as wrong or unfair, a bit of our personal power is lost. Our experience changes and we stop feeling happy and calm. Instead, we become upset and annoyed, which isn't good for us. Our blood pressure and heart rate increase as hormones (such as adrenalin and cortisol) are released in our bodies. Over a period of time, these physical reactions have adverse effects on our bodies.

Our bodies have a built-in "fight-or-flight" response. When angry, frightened, or otherwise stressed, we automatically produce hormones that let us put up a good fight—as in kill or disable our opponent—or help us escape.

When I was young, one of my weekly chores was to cut the grass. One hot summer day, I unexpectedly found a hornet's nest in our backyard. While dumping the grass clippings in a container behind the garage, I accidentally disturbed the nest, and what seemed to be a million hornets took issue with my presence. Everywhere I looked, I saw hornets—and it looked like they were preparing to attack. I remember running across the back yard like a gazelle. I felt like I was flying; my feet barely touched the ground. That was, without a doubt, the fastest I ever ran in my entire life. Many times afterwards, I tried to run with the same speed as I did that day, but never could. When I learned about adrenalin, I understood why I had such speed and dexterity that day and that day only.

Our basic—and essential—fight-or-flight mechanism is perfectly suited to yesterday's cavemen and cavewomen. However, these instinctive responses serve us poorly when we're confronted with unreasonable and ill-mannered individuals (or if we're challenged in a creative jewelry workshop). They also don't help if we're surprised by a negative response to a sincere friendly greeting. And they most certainly don't do us any good when dealing with crazy drivers and traffic. It's clear that it's not always in our best interest to confront someone when we're upset.

ONE REACTION AFTER ANOTHER

Every personal encounter involves an exchange of emotions, which we react to physically. Sometimes we feel great after seeing somebody, but other times we're ready to scream. That's why you can begin the day in a reasonably good mood and lose it after only one encounter with a hostile person. A steady diet of stress is harmful to both physical and mental health—and to our overall wellbeing.

It comes down to the emotions we transmit and receive during each interaction. Emotions are contagious—and are deeply related to personal power. People who interact positively are using their personal power in a beneficial way.

They exhibit a high level of self-awareness. They know how to manage their emotions and keep them in check. Rather than reacting negatively in challenging situations, they keep their calm. They don't blow up or stomp out of the room or leave other people with negative feelings. They control what they can: themselves.

If you deal with other people, this book is for you.
If you deal with yourself, this book is for you.

WHAT IS PERSONAL POWER?

Take the example we used above: a rude stranger stormed right through that door you held open. You thought he should've thanked you. When he didn't, you became angry—you gave some of your personal power away. Is it even logical that this annoying man had the power to trash your day just by showing up at your office door? Or was this a case of self-sabotaging reactive thinking?

I want to be clear about what I mean by *personal power*. After studying this issue—and enjoying some hard-won progress in the area—I define personal power as *having a high level of self-awareness about our reactions to others*. At its core, personal power means knowing, at a deep level, what is in the realm of our control, what is outside of our control, and accepting it.

Control is a key concept here. The word "control" itself has negative connotations: it sometimes implies the attempt to harmfully manipulate other people. For centuries, philosophers and social scientists have examined the use and misuse of power, often equating it with evil. Much of human history includes tragic and destructive tales of power being used to grab control over people, land, resources, and even religion.

We commonly see examples of misused power, authority, and even expertise. We need look no further than Bernie Madoff for an example of the misuse of *referent* power. Found guilty of running a colossal Ponzi scheme a few years ago, Mr. Madoff owned and operated Bernard L. Madoff Investments Securities, LLC. The firm functioned as a securities broker/dealer for individual investors and successful companies. A 2008 article in *The Economist* described Mr. Madoff's pedigree as top notch: "a pioneering marketer, he had chaired the NASDAQ stock exchange, had advised the government on market issues and was a noted philanthropist." And he consistently generated returns of 10% or more for his clients—regardless of market or economic conditions. Mr. Madoff was perceived to be an expert in his field, and even though his investment results were mathematically impossible, he was never questioned.

Harry Marcopolos, an unknown Boston accountant, questioned Mr. Madoff's calculations and tried to "blow the whistle" on him numerous times prior to 2008. But because of Madoff's powerful reputation, nobody—not even the Securities and Exchange Commission—listened to Marcopolos's warnings. In his book, *No One Would Listen: A True Financial Thriller,* Marcopolos said, "[They thought] I was a math geek and ignored my many protestations." In the end, many people gave away their personal power—and their entire life savings. Knowing that consistently earning that much money is impossible, the investors should've questioned the results and asked what their money was being used for. It appears that Mr. Madoff flexed his personal power more than his clients did, and to dishonest ends.

How many people are afraid to ask their doctor questions? We might say that we don't want to bother our doctor with our silly complaints, but most of the time we're intimidated by the implied power of the doctor and allow ourselves to be rushed. While still working in nuclear medicine, I had a patient who once went in for a check-up. His doctor wrote "R/O Gall

Bladder disease" on a prescription pad, presented it to him, and suggested he take it to the Radiology Department at the hospital. The man, obviously shaken, rushed to the department. With terror in his voice, he demanded that someone explain "R/O Gall Bladder disease" to him. "Exactly what is it, and is there a cure?"

The radiology receptionist very calmly explained to him that R/O was medical shorthand for Rule Out. The physician wanted us to rule out gall bladder disease. When asked why he didn't ask his physician to demystify the prescription message, the man responded, "He was just too busy, and I didn't want to bother him or take up his time." The man went through a terrible experience because he didn't want to ask his physician a question. He certainly gave away his power. Every time we behave in a way against our best interest, we give away our power.

We often view power in a positive light. Consumers have great power to influence the marketplace and create demand for products and services; voters have the power of the ballot box: the "power of the people." Many great moments in human history are attributed to the positive actions of average people who exercised their collective power. Examples include the 1773 Boston Tea Party, women suffrage, labor rights, racial equality, civil rights, environmental protection, and women's rights—up to and including today's Republican Tea Party movement. Sometimes this power took the form of direct action protests, such as marches, rallies, boycotts, and strikes. Other times it took the form of letters, petitions, public meetings, and election campaigns. People can create tremendous change when they collectively use their power.

These dimensions of power are worth studying, but this book is about *personal* power: what it is, how to know when you're giving it away, and what you need in order to take it back. I wrote this book for people of all ages and both genders. It's for managers and supervisors, business owners and employees, teachers and students. It's for anyone with family, loved ones, friends, or neighbors. It's for all of us who shop, drive, fly, use banks, go to the movies, or work out in a health club. It applies to anyone who has contact with other people. So, unless you're an exception to the rule—a hermit—you'll find a nugget or two of useful information.

MEET WYDIWYG™

I know what you're thinking—who the heck is that?

WYDIWYG (pronounced *wih-dee-wig*) is an acronym for **What You Do Is What You Get**. I created this in response to a question I've been asked so many times: *Why should I be the one who's nice?*

The reason is simple: we feel better when we're positive and pleasant. In fact, Dan Goleman tells us that our brains are "hard wired" to connect with and mimic others' emotions.

This means that our reactions to others, and theirs to us, have a tremendous biological impact on us. Hormones that regulate everything from our hearts to our immune systems are triggered when we connect face-to-face or voice-to-voice with someone else. Therefore, every encounter influences each person's emotional state. This is how "emotion exchange" works, day in and day out.

If we see someone who is laughing or happy, we often feel better ourselves; conversely, some people seem to take all the air out of a room. Emotions are contagious. On any given day, we connect and react to others, and they to us. In one way or another, virtually everything else in this book comes back to WYDIWYG. It's a very important concept.

> *What You Do Is What You Get*™
> – Kay Potetz, Ph.D.

Our actions and reactions reflect our understanding of personal power. That's what this book is all about: *your personal power*—and finding a way to take it back and live a happier life. The following chapters are about understanding personal power and looking at the many ways in which we give it away.

2

I NEVER SAW IT COMING

> *The true test in life does not occur when all is going well. The true test takes place when we are faced with challenges.*
> — CATHERINE PULSIFER, FROM ALL IS GOING WELL

Things go wrong in our lives, and we all make mistakes. To paraphrase John Steinbeck, sometimes even our best-laid plans go awry. Occasionally these glitches are small and only require minor course corrections, but some of our setbacks feel like full-body blows from which we'll never recover. Perhaps someone isn't as cooperative as we think they should be, or a conflict ends on a deeply unpleasant note. In a flash, unkind words are exchanged and comments made that are hard to forget.

Because of our instinctive fight-or-flight response, we react to challenging situations and threatening people by trying to protect ourselves. This behavior can be automatic and without regard for the psychological or physiological effects on ourselves or other people involved. Our basic human goal is survival; when our reactions are mechanical, we might not even know what set us off. We certainly won't have full control of our actions.

Take this example: Just yesterday you arrived home tired, annoyed, and frazzled. When your spouse or housemate asked about your day, you quickly responded with, "It was lousy," or "Don't even ask . . ." When this well-meaning person quickly walked away, you felt irritated and sulky.

You couldn't put your finger on the exact reason your day was so bad, but you were relieved it was over. You flopped in a chair, ready to relax as best you could. That lasted about two minutes. Then the kids descended on you, asking for money for a baseball game and a trip to the movies. After all, you *promised* they could go out with their friends. Your spouse wanted to rush through dinner to leave time for the two of you to take a ride to the auto dealership to look at new cars—never mind that you don't think the family can afford a car right now. Your youngest child was excited because his grandparents are coming for the weekend. Ah, yes, you'd tried to put that out of your mind. The prospects for a relaxing evening quickly vanished, and all you really wanted was an hour alone in a hot bath or channel surfing on the couch. The weekend wasn't looking so good either.

Okay, this is a fairly negative scenario. Perhaps you really do like your job and cherish your family. However, in various ways, you unknowingly spent your day relinquishing a lot of your power to others. You unwittingly allowed other people to trigger your anger and influence your decisions. Even small reactions stole your energy and left you feeling drained. If your day is like a boat, then you wasted your time in the harbor instead of sailing it to your destination. You became preoccupied with other things—leaving your personal power trailing behind in the wake. It happened so fast that you never saw it coming.

When I consult with clients or speak to audiences about personal power, every now and then someone reacts with a bit of an edge. "So what? If I want to complain about bad drivers or lazy employees, who is she to spoil my fun?" They like griping and grousing—it revs them up and makes them feel powerful. Some people are committed to misery.

This is where WYDIWYG—What You Do Is What You Get—can provide meaning and context. Many people are surprised to learn that this "revved-up" feeling is actually a result of increased heart rate and elevated blood pressure. At the University of Alabama, psychologist Dolf Zillman found that rage is similar to excitement: it "fosters the illusion of power and invulnerability that may inspire and facilitate aggression." The enraged person, "failing cognitive guidance," falls back on the most primitive of responses, i.e., fight-or-flight. It happens before we can control ourselves, and like a caffeine or sugar jolt, the energy rush can create a crashing wave of fatigue. These physiological reactions are simply a waste of valuable energy, and self-generated stress causes real physical damage. We give away our power—and our health—with these kinds of negative responses.

Everyone can recall times when they reacted to other people's actions with disappointment, hurt, anger, or deep agitation. We rerun contentious conversations in a loop in our heads, or we think of clever retorts that should've rolled off our tongue. Why, oh why didn't we think of that at the time? Perhaps we failed to land the job or client we wanted.

We can't let go of the idea that we were cheated somehow—that someone else failed to see our true merits. We waste our energy revisiting the past and wishing for a different outcome, clinging to a moment that's dead and gone.

Growing up and becoming autonomous involves making decisions about what appeals to us—and what doesn't—in all areas of life, from careers to cars to shoes. These choices develop our individuality and exercise our personal awareness and power. On the other hand, our choices don't necessarily imply a judgment about the things we don't choose. Just because I drive a red car doesn't mean I judge those who drive blue cars.

Take It Back refers specifically to the personal power we give away to others, every day of our lives. For example, as we discussed in Chapter 1, how do you respond when someone carelessly cuts in front of you on the road? Do you waste your energy by stomping on the accelerator and rushing to pass the offender? Do you brashly cut in front of him to give him a taste of his own medicine? Agitation and anger shrink your ability to think rationally and make good decisions. Road rage raises your blood pressure, which might go up again if you tell other people about the incident (and what that other driver "made you do"). The response is automatic: you're unsettled, you've given away your power, and you never saw it coming.

What if you let your annoyance—and fear—pass? You'll stop chewing over it. By repeating that moment in your mind, you give it an energy—and a shelf life—that it doesn't deserve. Life is more fulfilling, less disappointing, and certainly less irritating if we stop giving away our power to others. Instead, we must hang on to our power and value it.

LEARNING FROM EXPERIENCE—MAYBE

Today I have a good understanding of my personal power. I know that I'm totally in charge of my day. Reality is neutral, and it's up to me to put a positive or negative spin on whatever happens. Like most people, though, I developed this knowledge—this way of being and thinking—over time and through self-observation. I discovered a feedback loop that showed me how much happier and more productive my life can be when I own and honor my personal power. If I react negatively to other people, or claim that everything would be wonderful if not for someone's actions, I'm giving my power away—and no good ever comes from that.

I've also learned not to expect certain responses from others. For example, if you greet someone with a big smile and get one in return, you'll go happily about your business. But let's say the person doesn't smile back. You'll be disappointed, and maybe that turns into frustration. Before you know it, you're analyzing and crafting explanations for why they're being so rude. You created an expectation, and when it's unfulfilled, you start down the road of giving your power away. Some folks make rigid, judgmental conclusions about rude behavior and leave it at that. Others waste their time analyzing and trying to understand the reasons for the incident. Either way, personal power is sacrificed.

Many things can trigger this grim journey into judgment and analysis. Maybe you did a favor for a coworker that helped her shine, but she never properly thanked you or recognized your contribution to her success. Will you waste time and energy on the path of "shoulds" and "oughts?" She *should* have offered her thanks, and you really *ought* to teach her a thing or two about office manners. Whether you lose a few minutes or several hours, no matter how long you mull it over, you've given away your power to something over which you have no control.

Don't should on me

Recall a time in your life when you were let down by something someone did or didn't do. It could be as small as an unreturned smile or a courtesy gone unnoticed. Whatever it was, you thought the other person failed to do the right thing. Weren't you disappointed? Perhaps you even admitted that you were angry or had hurt feelings. But in your mind, their behavior was the catalyst that brought on your pain.

Frustrated expectations underlie your feelings. You anticipated something from that other person, but you were dissatisfied when you never got it. Maybe you were wrong in your judgment. Maybe you were truly disappointed in the person. But the majority of us do this routinely—and we're completely unaware of it.

Do people learn from these experiences? I'd like to say yes, but the real answer is "not usually." We're creatures of habit; therefore, most of us repeat what we know and fail to change unproductive behavior. We expect people to act a certain way, but when they surprise us, we share our anger and dissatisfaction with anyone who'll listen. We do this all day long, and every time we revisit the stressful event, our bodies physically suffer.

To avoid being trapped in this reaction, try raising your level of self-awareness. Become aware of your triggers, and learn what sets you off. For example, do you expect people to always use manners? I can almost hear you saying, "All I'm asking for is a simple *thank you*." And I understand how you feel, but know that some people leave their proper etiquette at home, never had any to begin with, or perhaps express appreciation at an inaudible level. Self-awareness of our desire to receive thanks—knowing that some folks are incapable of providing it—prepares us for these annoying moments in life. I hold the door for someone because it's the right thing to do, not because I expect a "thank you" in return. I maintain my personal power because I always see these minor—but dangerous—incidents coming. By clearly identifying life's irritations, we can develop techniques that allow us to safely ignore them.

3

ASSUMPTIONS, ATTITUDES, AND BELIEFS

> *Your assumptions are your windows on the world. Scrub them off every once and a while or the light won't come in.*
>
> — **Alan Alda**

As you go about your day, you probably don't spend much time thinking about your personal beliefs. However, your beliefs shape your behavior in countless ways: they determine how you interact with others at work and at home, how you spend your time off, and even what's in your closet. In terms of personal power, our beliefs help us to either keep or lose our *internal* power. We can give power away externally, through interactions with other people, but it's just as important to understand how we give away power *internally*.

To start with, we carry around beliefs about ourselves that guide our behavior. We build up habits to support our beliefs and keep them alive. But our habits can both support us and sabotage us. Further, we part with our assumptions about ourselves only reluctantly, if at all. Let me explain.

I teach in the MBA program at Baldwin Wallace College, a small liberal arts college located southwest of Cleveland, Ohio. In 2002 I taught a class, "Behavioral Theories of Management," with Dr. Harry Bury, a psychologist who graduated from Case Western Reserve University. Harry is quite a character, and I always enjoy team-teaching with him. Harry believed that in some circumstances, embarrassment can be switched into humor. He called it "reframing": we can choose to look through a different lens and find the humor in any situation. I've used his theory many times. For example, one day while having lunch with friends, one of my lunch-mates glanced down at my shoes and, with a puzzled look on her face, said, "Your shoes don't match."

"They certainly do," I hastily replied. "My shoes are brown and my clothes have various shades of brown in them. Everything matches!"

She rolled her eyes and said, "I mean your shoes don't match each other. You're wearing two different brown shoes."

I sheepishly looked down at my feet. She was right. My shoes didn't match each other.

The choice was mine: I could be embarrassed and attempt a feeble explanation for my mismatched shoes ("My bedroom was dark when I dressed that morning"), or I could relax and find humor in the situation. I chose the latter and said, "You know, I have a pair just like these at home."

With that, we all started laughing and enjoyed the rest of our meal. Finding humor in situations is a very powerful response.

The class I taught with Harry spent a great deal of time on the study of perceptions and self-awareness. It was particularly illuminating to understand that most of us are more aware of others' behaviors and beliefs than our own. We spend considerable time watching and assessing the way other people live, work, play, and react. But how much time do we spend examining our own attitudes and beliefs, which influence every action and decision we will make in our lives?

Have you ever caught yourself giving advice to a friend, but, in your mind's eye, red flags are waving wildly? The red flag is a flash of self-awareness, telling you that maybe you should apply this advice to yourself! You're an expert when it comes to others—how your friend should solve a relationship problem or find a better job or ask for a raise—but what about your barely viable relationship with your sister or your boredom with your job?

Many of us even tell others how they should or shouldn't feel or assure them that a problem isn't nearly as bad as it might seem. But how do we know what's really happening in their lives? Besides, your advice can't change anything about the other person's situation.

Because most of us aren't in touch with the power we have over our thoughts and beliefs, it's challenging to understand our actions and why we say the things we say. Remember that reality is neutral, but human nature isn't. We see and hear what we want and need, and we try to fix a meaning to everything that happens in our lives.

What one individual disdains, another holds dear. There's an old saying: *It all depends on whose ox is being gored.*

No two people see things in the same way—let alone have identical feelings. Is the glass half empty or half full? We have a tremendous power: to select what we see. And though we can't always change the world into what we want, we can select the lens through which we view it. Altering our perceptions is one way to retrieve personal power, but in order to succeed, we must first sharpen our self-awareness.

Daniel Goleman refers to self-awareness as "an ongoing attention to one's internal states." Therefore, self-awareness is directly related to our thoughts and emotions. For example, some individuals are easily overwhelmed by emotion, while others barely notice even high-impact events. I once worked with an excellent RN who lost a glove while riding the bus. She was distraught for days. Her favorite pair of gloves was ruined, and she kept on berating herself for losing them. On the other hand, I have a cousin whose car was stolen. He reacted with next to no emotion. He simply shrugged his shoulders and said, "Well, it was insured."

Both reactions fall on the extreme ends of the emotional spectrum. However, these examples illustrate how we can control our thoughts, feelings and emotions.

Harry had an amusing way of describing how we can raise our levels of self-awareness and grasp the power we have over our thoughts. Go with me on this, and let yourself play with the images that come to mind. According to Harry, a "nitwit" lives in your head—and he's always busy.

Imagine that you have two rows of file cabinets inside your head—one row in the front, the other in back. Each file cabinet holds hundreds, even thousands, of 3" x 5" index cards. (Remember those?) The cabinets in the front hold cards filled with notations about every negative thing that has ever happened to you. The cards in the back list all your positive experiences. Everything you've ever seen, heard, felt, or done is duly noted on an index card and stored in either the positive or negative file.

In your "brain office," there is a hardworking nitwit who will do anything you ask. His job is to follow your orders, and he has no particular feeling or opinion about the value of any order you give him. The orders could be good for you, or, just as likely, they could be detrimental. He's oblivious—that's why Harry called him the nitwit.

For example, if you say to yourself, "I don't think I can do that," the nitwit shuffles through the negative files until he comes up with a card that proves, sure enough, you can't do whatever "that" is. He pulls out the card and says, "You're right, boss. You messed this up last year. You probably can't do that."

If, on the other hand, you say to yourself, "I think I can do this," he makes a beeline for the positive file located in the back of your head and plucks a card to support that thought. "You certainly can, boss," he says. "You did it before, and you can do it again." Your head tips down when the nitwit goes to the negative files in the front of your brain, but your head tips up when the nitwit is busy in positive files at the back of your brain.

If you want a good quality of life, with all kinds of positive experiences, it's your job to keep the nitwit in the back files. Pay attention to which way your head is tipping, so you know the exact location of your nitwit at any given time.

Harry referred to the nitwit as "he," but if it helps you to conceptualize your self-talk or automatic responses, then by all means give him or *her* a name, or picture a gremlin or other "stand-in" character in your mind. But the point remains the same: you have total control over how your nitwit spends his time. You can control your thoughts.

THE NITWIT IN ACTION

Every day, we give voice to our nitwit through a barrage of self-talk. For example, let's say a friend invites you to a lecture and slideshow at a nearby library. The topic is new discoveries in space, and your first reaction is positive—the nitwit flies to the index cards that say: *I like lectures, and I like space. Plus, the library isn't far away, and I especially enjoy the company of that particular friend.*

So far, so good. Then your friend tells you the lecture is on Thursday *night*. In the blink of an eye, the nitwit dives to the front of the brain and yanks a card that says: *I can't drive at night.* What a bummer, you think. Now you'll have to say no.

Maybe your friend says, "Oh, I forgot about you and night driving. I usually don't mention evening events because I figure you'll always say no."

You end the phone call, disappointed.

What just happened? To start with, the nitwit stays busy digesting information you have fed it over a lifetime, and it faithfully acts on your orders. In this case, he acted without a glitch to manage your thoughts and behaviors based on your key entrenched beliefs. On the one hand, you enjoy science and space, and on the other hand you fear driving at night.

What comes next? You might resent the library for scheduling such interesting events at night. *Why couldn't they invite the space scientist to speak on a Saturday afternoon? Saturdays are much more convenient. More people would show up if they held it on Saturday, or better yet, Sunday afternoon.*

By the time you're done, you're ready to write a letter to the library board or the newspaper. You're not so thrilled with your friend either. It's her fault, after all, for telling you about the lecture in the first place.

This negative outcome is made possible by one belief: *I can't drive at night.* Right on cue, the nitwit waved the index card at you, and because you listen to this kind of self-talk, your self-defeating thoughts ruled the day. You relinquished your own personal power for a belief that may not be valid and whose source you might never have truly examined.

Of course, certain health conditions affect vision and the ability to drive at night. But the story above is just an example of the kinds of beliefs that trap us in old patterns and habits. Let's say the person in our last example doesn't have any particular reason not to drive at night. Perhaps it was a habit based on the fact that her parents stopped driving after dark at about age sixty. Why? Well, she isn't sure why. It was something they believed was right, and now she believes it, too. Apparently, she doesn't believe in taking taxis or buses at night either!

BELIEFS BY THE THOUSANDS

Our beliefs can move us forward in life or they can hold us back. – Oprah Winfrey, 2000

The "I can't drive at night" belief is one of thousands of notes on index cards in the filing cabinets, both back and front. Of course, our self-talk reinforces positive beliefs, too. For example:

- Ellen jumps at the chance to play on the company softball team. Her colleagues laugh at her, but they don't know she played softball in college. She believes she can get her skills back. Besides, she likes to have fun.
- Barry expects the best from his employees, and he reciprocates their loyalty by treating them with respect. Last week, Barry walked out of the local small business owners meeting because he grew weary of all the managers griping about their lazy employees.
- Susan believes every child in her classroom has aptitudes and talents, and she always finds unique qualities in each child.
- Self-talk also reinforces negative beliefs:
- Alex always thought she was smarter than her sister, Tina. Alex also complains about how Tina is stubborn as a mule. When Tina opened a business, Alex just *knew* it would fail. Sure enough, the first few months were a real bust. But stubborn Tina wouldn't face facts, though, and she fought hard to overcome the rough start. Then a year later, when Tina expanded the business, Alex congratulated Tina on being lucky.
- Patrick is stuck in a job with no opportunities for promotion. Over the years, Patrick has seen many coworkers leave for better jobs—but not

him. He stays put, thinking that the best path to job security is to keep the job he has and build up long years of seniority. Those who leave for better jobs are much more vulnerable to layoffs, he thinks. Imagine Patrick's dismay when his company went out of business during a severe economic downturn.

- Joe doesn't like people of particular ethnic backgrounds. He regularly talks about all the ways they're inferior and vehemently rejects all opposing information. His mind is made up.

Mind you, people with positive self-talk in some areas can still be negative in others. Ellen might avoid public speaking at all costs because she performed poorly in grade school assemblies; thus, she loses personal power to that belief. Joe might be confident in his abilities at math, which got him a good job in an accounting department.

In all the above examples, the nitwit comes into play. Ellen's nitwit raced to the file cabinet for old softball experiences, while Joe's nitwit waits for the chance to endlessly shuffle through his file of biases and prejudices.

WE'RE CREATURES OF HABIT

Our beliefs, our behavior, and our habits are all connected. We'll repeat our behavior and create a supporting structure of habits to support our beliefs—even if we lose personal power because of them. If we decide we can't drive at night, then we'll build a lifestyle around this belief and may even draw our friends into it. Before long, our family and friends will believe that we prefer to stay home, and they'll stop including us in their plans. Our habits perpetuate our beliefs, especially if we never stop to examine the source.

On the other hand, when Barry decided to leave a meeting that had turned into a gripe session about employees, it was because he'd built habits around his belief in his own employees. He organizes his manufacturing plant around teams; he lets his employees enforce safety standards, juggle schedules, and correct production errors using their own judgment. Barry's attitudes reflect trust and high expectations, which he believes made his business so successful. His parents owned a business and ran it the same way, so he grew up viewing employees as assets rather than liabilities. If Barry had stayed for lunch, he knew he'd start arguing with others at his lunch table and leave upset. He understood that distress is a loss of internal personal power. That time, he removed himself from the situation instead.

Our friend Alex has a strong belief in her own intelligence—good for her. Too bad she also believes that one sister has to be smarter than the other, and that she designated herself to fill that role. This is typical within families, and rigid habits often form around assigned family roles. Tina bravely reexamined a belief she carried from childhood into her adult life: "I'm not destined for the smashing success that Alex achieved." This belief had left her internally weak and unsure of herself—certainly lacking a sense of internal personal power. But because Tina longed to own a business, she was willing to transform her old belief. As a result, she managed to fight through some tough startup months. Alex likes to prove herself right, so she obviously attributed Tina's success to luck. To do otherwise would mean admitting she was wrong.

Patrick's beliefs around job security remind us of what used to be known as the "Depression mentality"—which doesn't refer to a clinical condition. Patrick's father lived through the Great Depression of the 1930s, and he taught Patrick to find a secure job and hang onto it at all costs. Times changed, but

Patrick clung to that old belief about job security, which suppressed his sense of internal power over his own choices. It worked for a while, but his company's bankruptcy changed everything. To avoid feeling like a victim, Patrick must reexamine the belief that had kept him working at a job he disliked—and lost anyway.

Ellen might have great confidence in her softball skills, but she decided that she *can't* speak to groups. She developed habits that allow her to avoid any form of public speaking, even to the point that she refused to chair a committee at her church to avoid delivering a report to the congregation. Ellen doesn't understand that she's built much of her life around her fear; after all, she's a social person and close to her family. She's the librarian-researcher at a large law firm, perfectly suited to her comfort zone because no one will ever ask her to deliver a speech.

We all know folks like Joe. Bias and prejudice are usually born in childhood and develop by osmosis. Some people pick up family beliefs about certain groups or religions, which might be reinforced through neighbors and classmates. Fortunately, in our society, many people work hard to examine and overcome their prejudices, and young people routinely point out the backward thinking of the older generation. But then there's Joe, who protects his beliefs through a series of habits. In order to keep his job, he doesn't talk about his opinions at work, but he has prejudiced friends (and a long email list) with whom he feels "safe." He likes nothing better than telling stories that "prove" his point about this or that group.

That brings us to Susan, who represents the power of expectations. Some have called this the "Pygmalion Effect," and it's the theme of the next chapter.

4

THE PYGMALION EFFECT: YOU GET WHAT YOU EXPECT

> *People are always blaming circumstances for what they are. I don't believe in circumstances. The people who get on in the world are the people who get up and look for the circumstances they want, and if they can't find them, make them.*
> — GEORGE BERNARD SHAW

The Pygmalion Effect tells us that expectations or beliefs determine behavior and performance. It's a self-fulfilling prophecy that helps make our expectations come true. In the last chapter, I mentioned Susan, a teacher who believed that each of her students arrived in her classroom with unique qualities. Her job as a teacher involved discovering and nurturing these qualities, and year after year, her belief produced the Pygmalion Effect. If Susan had focused on negative qualities—telling her students that they were lazy or dumb or impossible to teach—her classroom would probably misbehave and perform poorly.

The term "Pygmalion Effect" has historical roots in the Greek myth about the sculptor Pygmalion. He claimed to hate women, but he fell in love with an ivory statue of a beautiful woman he'd carved himself. Eventually, he became so infatuated with the statue that he prayed to the goddess Aphrodite to bring her to life. The goddess heard his prayer, granted his wish, and Pygmalion's statue did indeed come to life.

George Bernard Shaw's play *Pygmalion* is an adaptation of the ancient myth, and the 1960s movie *My Fair Lady*, based on the play, is still considered a classic. If you haven't seen it, it's worth your time to rent the DVD. Arrogant and ignorant about women, Rex Harrison transforms—in short order—an awkward, Cockney-accented Audrey Hepburn into an elegant beauty with aristocratic manners. He works his miracles because he believed in her, and in her way, of course, she transforms him as well.

We can see how the essence of the Pygmalion Effect applies to everyday situations. People's beliefs and expectations of themselves have a tremendous effect on both behavior and results. For example, I have friends who tell me they can never lose weight, and—you guessed it—they can't. They might try every diet on the planet, and sometimes they'll even see a bit of improvement. But their belief of ultimate failure is overpowering, which translates to zero weight loss and sometimes into weight gain. If you say to yourself, "That's me," I invite you to begin an analysis of your thoughts. Observe what you say when you talk to yourself. Remember the nitwit in your head, who finds data to support whatever you believe. We often say things to ourselves that we'd never say to our friends and loved ones.

I frequently observe students failing classes they could have easily passed had they maintained a positive mindset and believed in their abilities. Instead, they fixate on their inabilities. Many learners are willing to be coached, and they transition into a positive mindset once they enjoy success. But a few seem committed to failure.

I have a thirty-year-old cousin who chose not to attend college; he'd convinced himself that he was simply not a student. But this past year, after twelve years of demanding physical labor, he decided he wanted to go to college. He told me that he had a great interest in working in the health care field, given that it was one of the few areas of the economy still hiring. He's a gentle soul and will do quite well—health care always has room for caring people. However, he was hesitant to pursue his dream because he believed he was ill-equipped in the area of math. Or more specifically, "I suck in math" (his words). Matt's fear of failure was probably what prevented him from going to college years ago. He'd convinced himself of his inability because he did poorly in high school.

Fortunately, he was open to suggestions, and eventually he altered his mindset. He stopped declaring himself "no good in math." Instead, he expected positive things from himself and started night school at Cuyahoga Community College. At the time of this writing, he has a 4.0 (A) average. Whether or not he finishes his degree is his choice, but at least he no longer believes that he's too dumb for college. I'm always amazed when people make decisions and then do everything in their power to support them. Depending on the decisions we make, our efforts can be for good or for bad.

You move toward that upon which you focus. —Kay Potetz, Ph.D.

In order to graduate at Baldwin Wallace, all business majors are required to take "Strategy and Policy." This senior-level course makes use of a computer game that simulates running a company. Students are divided into teams and compete with each other for market share, advertising results, profits, and so forth. The game is a reproduction of the real business world, and students must be familiar with accounting procedures, marketing plans, and staffing requirements.

Most students have fun and learn with the game; unfortunately, one or two folks always have a real fear of failing and not graduating with their class. They waste their energy convincing themselves that they don't understand the material and that they're going to fail. Once they commit to this thought, unfortunately, they live out their expectations—failing the class and being forced to retake it in summer school.

In the professional world, this example has profound implications for those we work *with* and work *for*. Their opinions of our abilities, skills, and capacities greatly affect our productivity, output, and overall quality of experience on the job.

I once conducted a seminar at an extended care facility in the Greater Cleveland area. The owner's goal was to implement a new and improved customer relations program with an emphasis on staff members' interpersonal skills and ability to communicate with others. As Gary, the owner, succinctly put it: "They're very good at what they do, but I want them to show a softer side, you know, more humanness."

Numerous studies indicate that an organization's *informal* leaders have tremendous powers of persuasion, and fellow employees often mimic their behavior. After much discussion, the facility's management team finally agreed that the program would best succeed if a group of influential employees spread the positive message to others.

The managers created a list of individuals identified as informal leaders, and those employees were *invited* to attend the meeting. (Attendance was actually mandatory, but the notice was presented as an invitation.) As the room filled, I observed the usual display of employee attitudes: some showed a degree of openness and curiosity; others were annoyed by having to attend another meeting; and some were clearly bored with the whole idea. They were probably uninterested because, in their experience, meetings were always a waste of time. Their body language communicated feelings of downright resistance, that "it's the same old dumb stuff again." You know what I mean: a lot of folks sitting with their arms crossed and not one person wearing a smile.

When Gary addressed the group, he received typical, perfunctory attention until he said, "The management team and

I have selected all of you for this project." The operative word was selected. Gary went on to explain to these employees—who were now paying close attention—that management picked them because they'd been identified as the informal leaders in the facility. "You are men and women that others look up to and admire," he said, "so we believe that if you carry the message about our new customer relations program to your co-workers, it will be a great success."

Like the sun breaking through the clouds after a five-day downpour, the room brightened, body language changed, and a dramatic transformation occurred. In an instant, the room became charged with excitement: everyone in the group suddenly showed great interest in the program and a willingness to participate. Soon they were offering their own ideas and bonding together like comrades on a secret mission. This example illustrates the Pygmalion Effect in action—and the group ascended to the highest level of the manager's expectations.

GREATER EXPECTATIONS

The situation at the extended care facility reminded me of a study conducted years ago by the Chicago Public School System, in which researchers recruited a group of teachers to participate. The teachers were told that they were picked for the study because of their excellent teaching abilities, and further, that gifted students would be placed in their classrooms. The researchers designed the study to find out how students would perform if they were unaware of their special status; neither the children nor their parents were told about the study.

As the teachers expected, the children showed exceptional scholastic performance. In addition, the teachers told the researchers that working with the gifted children was a delight and that they'd welcome the opportunity to do so again. At that point, the researchers informed the teachers that the children were not necessarily gifted. In fact, they were chosen at random from all the students in Chicago's schools. The teachers also learned that they, too, had been randomly chosen.

The researchers named this remarkable outcome "The Pygmalion Effect in the Classroom." Robert Rosenthal and Lenore Jacobson expanded the study into a book, *Pygmalion in the Classroom: Teacher Expectation and Pupils' Intellectual Development*. The teachers' high expectations for the supposedly gifted students, though never officially expressed, influenced the children to believe in themselves and act accordingly. The teachers rose to the occasion as well, thus living up to the "honor" of being chosen for the task.

This study gained a great deal of attention, and other research also confirmed that—at least to some degree—people rise or fall to the level of others' expectations. This means that the Pygmalion Effect applies broadly to every area of life.

Did you ever notice that there are people with whom you naturally feel comfortable? It takes no effort on your part to spend time with them. Usually, these folks think your ideas are great. You express yourself clearly when you talk to them; your words ring with clarity and insight. This special rapport comes from their belief that you're bright. If you know people have positive beliefs about you, you're more likely to work hard and make sure your ideas live up to their expectations.

We've also experienced the opposite phenomenon. There are individuals with whom we're uncomfortable, even uneasy, who we think don't like us. We avoid these people and perform poorly when they're present; we may be halting and hesitant and less articulate. We believe they're labeling us negatively, which makes us feel like victims. We're usually less likely to engage in persuasive conversation to get them to understand our point of view.

In their book, *Dealing with People You Can't Stand*, Drs. Rick Brinkman and Rick Kirschner use the term *Pygmalion Power*. As an example, parents wield Pygmalion Power if they tell their children: *If I've told you once, I've told you a thousand times! You're:*

- messy;
- clumsy—an accident waiting to happen;
- a liar;
- lazy;
- a slob;
- good for nothing;
- self-centered—you don't care about anyone but yourself.

The parents get what they expect because the child's behavior conforms to this negative attitude. The more parents berate the child, the more the child acts out. This might be a common use of Pygmalion Power, but it's a poor use of a great tool. When used in a positive way, Pygmalion Power can bring out the best in people, even when they're at their worst. For example:

- Your teenage son looks messy, but instead of labeling him as a slob, you say, "That's not like you! You care about your appearance."
- Your eight-year-old behaves carelessly and breaks a toy. Rather than labeling her clumsy, you say, "This isn't like you. You know how to take care of things."
- Your child is failing math, and you know it's because he hasn't been studying very hard.

You could emphasize how lazy he's been, but instead you say, "You're capable of doing anything you put your mind to."

In other words, we choose the way we react to our children, as well as other relatives, friends, and coworkers. We can bring out their best when they've made mistakes by affirming that we know them to be caring individuals and expressing our love and concern for them.

THE PYGMALION EFFECT AT WORK

When we apply the Pygmalion Effect to management and work situations, the operative principle is *"other people's thoughts and beliefs about us, especially those individuals in authority positions, have an impact on our performance."* This has profound implications for working with and for other people, and it becomes clear that understanding the Pygmalion Effect is an important key to improving a workforce.

I'm reminded of Jerry, an orthopedic technician with whom I used to work. For those of you not familiar with hospital work, an orthopedic technician sets up and installs all the traction equipment—the trapeze, weights, and so forth—for patients undergoing bone surgery. Jerry was expected to arrive at work in the morning, check the surgery schedule, and set up the required traction equipment on the patients' beds. All of this had to be done prior to patients returning to their rooms after the surgical procedures were completed.

Jerry had worked in other hospital departments before. Not known as the best employee, he'd even been written up on occasion for poor behavior. The consensus was that Jerry was unmotivated and had to be closely watched because he had a tendency to goof off. Hospital staff treated him as though he was lazy and unaccountable. Of course, he lived up to their expectations.

Jerry would spend two hours avoiding a half-hour of work. He seemed to find challenge and enjoyment in ditching his responsibilities; frankly, he often succeeded. I watched him do this many times and grew increasingly annoyed. It seemed like he was playing a game.

This is a perfect example of me giving away *my* power: *I* was irritated because *he* was being lazy. But he was motivated enough to avoid his work with creativity and daring; all he needed to do was change his focus. Wouldn't his life be easier if he just completed his assignments? Thoughts ran through my mind: *Frankly I'm not all that motivated. When I get an assignment, I complete it to the best of my ability in as short of time as possible. I wouldn't dream of wasting time by trying to avoid what I need to do anyway.*

Not Jerry. His attitude seemed to be: *If I've got the name, I might as well play the game. Everyone thinks I'm lazy, so far be it from me to disappoint my co-workers.*

At the time, I was studying organizational behavior in graduate school. I wondered how he'd react if he was treated like an excellent employee instead. So I began complimenting Jerry when he performed well. I progressively gave him more responsibility and explained that I really counted on him. Slowly he started living up to my expectations, and his performance improved. Let me stress, this was a slow process; but as Jerry steadily got better, he eventually grew into a fine, reliable orthopedic technician. He lived up to my expectations, and guess what? I was spared from a life of irritation. I'd taken back my power from Jerry.

Management should do everything possible to give supervisors a highly positive attitude about their employees.

Employees should be encouraged to view their supervisors in the same way. Both supervisors and employees will then have faith in their organization's potential; in other words, the Pygmalion Effect will be experienced organization-wide. And as we shall see, the Pygmalion Effect is present in every interpersonal interaction.

In their book *Organizational Behavior,* Robert Kreitner and Angelo Kinicki provide suggestions on how to influence others to perform positively. They recommend using various combinations of the following:

- ✓ Recognize that everyone has the potential to increase his or her performance.
- ✓ Set high performance goals.
- ✓ Positively reinforce folks for a job well done.
- ✓ Provide constructive feedback when necessary.
- ✓ Introduce new employees as if they have outstanding potential.
- ✓ Become aware of your personal prejudices and nonverbal messages that may discourage others.

Consciously or not, we tip off people about our expectations. Our bodies exhibit thousands of cues, some as subtle as tilting the head, raising an eyebrow, or having dilated nostrils. Others pick up on these cues unconsciously, but most of our reactions, verbal and nonverbal, are much more obvious.

The Pygmalion Effect has enormous power to elevate behavior, not only in the workplace and in the classroom, but also in the way we relate to one another. The Pygmalion Effect also plays a role in how we explain our successes or failures—and the almost universal tendency to come up with excuses.

5

GOODBYE EXCUSES

> *When you blame others, you give up your power to change.*
> — ROBERT ANTHONY

Everyone needs to soothe their ailing psyche now and then. No one's life is free of disappointment, loss, or regret. We all have experienced the dull ache that comes from making a bad decision. How do you deal with life's uncertainties and disappointments? What do you say to yourself to ease the pain? Or, here's another question: whom or what do you blame when comforting yourself over the agony of failure or regret? Have you ever said, "Look what you made me do," or "I can't go if she refuses," or "What will they think if I'm not there?"

These comments probably sound very familiar, because when personal disaster strikes, our first inclination is to look outside of ourselves for explanations—or people to blame. Few of us will admit it, but we often hold others responsible for the poor outcomes of our decisions, actions, or bad habits.

I used to smoke cigarettes. Every now and then, someone gave me unsolicited advice about quitting (often bragging that they woke up one day and just quit, never to think about smoking again). They asked why I smoked, because, after all, it was bad for me. (Wow! Really?) But they were wasting their words. I knew exactly why I smoked: *both of my parents smoked*. Everything flowed from that. I forgot about my decision to try cigarette smoking in high school to fit in with other kids. Nor did I admit that, at one time, I thought smoking looked cool.

Internally or externally, I never once acknowledged that it was my decision to pick up the first cigarette—and the next 100, and the next 1,000—and that I was physically hooked on nicotine and the psychological crutch of smoking. I'd developed a terrible habit, but it had to be my parents' fault because both of them smoked.

My parents have since passed away, and I miss them terribly. But reflecting on their lives with more mature eyes, I confess that neither of them ever offered me a cigarette or invited me to join them in smoking. In fact, my dad often told me how disappointed he was that I had started; he encouraged me to quit, calling the habit expensive, dirty, and bad for my health. Did I listen? No! He and Mom were totally responsible for my smoking habit—that was my story and I stuck to it for at least ten years. Not only did I stick to it, I believed it.

> *The best years of your life are the ones in which you decide your problems are your own. You do not blame them on your mother, the ecology, or the president. You realize that you control your own destiny.*
> – Albert Ellis

When we scramble to place blame on someone—anyone—we're living in a metaphorical "house with no mirrors." And because of our decision to live there, we suffer from a bad case of *"Excusitis."* This serious, excuse-based disease robs us of our vital energy—our personal power—because we use up most of our drive battling the sickness. Without a few metaphorical mirrors hanging on the internal walls of your psyche, you can only defend yourself and blame others. With every excuse, another bit of personal power drains away.

How many mirrors do you have? If your internal house isn't furnished with an adequate number of mirrors, you'll never effectively identify the major symptoms of *Excusitis*. I coined the term a few years ago to describe people who always find others responsible for the troubles in their lives. I guess if we broke down the Latin, it would literally mean "inflammation of excuses," and we all know inflammation is painful.

FROM EXCUSE TO VICTIM

Excusitis propels us into the role of a victim. Show me a person who feels victimized whenever something goes wrong, and I'll show you a person who has ready-made excuses for everything. This kind of person lacks the self-awareness required for a high level of emotional intelligence (a concept that's discussed in greater detail in the next chapter).

THE SHAPES AND SIZES OF EXCUSES

Many of us don't stop long enough to really listen to ourselves. If we do, then the language of *Excusitis* becomes clear:

- Look what she made me do!
- He runs our lives, so I can't make a decision.
- My hands were tied.
- Poor me!
- I'm trapped at this company.
- She's always messing up and dragging me down.
- No one appreciates my contribution in . . . (the arts, the sciences, business, community affairs, etc.)
- He needs me, so I can't leave.
- My boss treats me worse than anyone else in the office.
- The market dropped—that's why I'm broke.

Fairytales, every one of them. Whether we resent our boss, hate our work, have marital problems, deal with unreliable friends, feel unappreciated, or face any other life challenges, telling and re-telling our story will bear us little fruit. It drains away our personal power and diverts us from the real issue. If we find ourselves bringing up one excuse after another, we need to hang some internal mirrors.

Those who speak the language of *Excusitis* and "victimology" often go from one from mess to another, reinforcing their strong belief that they're victims of circumstance. As long as they stay in that mental space, they remain unaware that they have the potential to change or improve their situation. In other words, they can't experience personal power, which would propel them into positive action.

THE PHONY UPSIDE OF VICTIMOLOGY

People with *Excusitis* often covet their condition. If we're always the injured party, then we can find ourselves innocent whenever anything bad happens. Perpetual victimhood relieves us of the burden of personal responsibility. Every lousy day is someone else's fault. How great is that!

Unfortunately, this state of so-called innocence is like living in a box. We can never really fail, but we can never go far. We can't achieve personal growth, reach goals, or enrich our lives when we rob ourselves of individual responsibility and action. Wasting our personal power on excuses leaves us unable to make decisions that advance our best interests.

DECISIONS, DECISIONS

How often do you look at your life today and trace things back to decisions you've made? If we're happy with our lives, we might point to "fate": the synchronicities that seemed, almost by magic, to let us progress and reach our goals. But if we're not happy, then we must be the victims of plain old bad luck.

To live fully, we need to assess the decisions we make along the way. You choose your spouse, friends, job, and living conditions, just like you choose whether to be upset by last night's newscast or your coworker's bad mood. This is an unpleasant fact if you're dissatisfied with your lot in life.

Being an adjunct, part-time professor, I conduct my classes in the evening. Most of my adult students are currently in the workforce, but decided to return to school to earn a bachelor's degree in business. I've experienced great pleasure by helping these students grow and achieve their goals. However, one specific student comes to mind—I'll call him Elmo.

The evening of our first class of a new semester, Elmo matter-of-factly told me he had an extremely full schedule, so he probably wouldn't complete his assignments on time. Furthermore, he was already working a full-time job and taking two other classes—not to mention his three small children at home. Oh, and one more thing: depending on the babysitter's schedule, he might have to miss a class or two.

Elmo believed that, since nothing could be done about his stressful situation and myriad hardships, I'd surely understand and support him through the next few months. Finally, he asked that I "cut him some slack" and be sympathetic when grading him.

Elmo's life certainly was a hectic state of affairs. Wow, three little kids, a full-time job, and other classes. I imagine Elmo's nerve-racking schedule left him pretty tired at the end of the day.

But what fascinated me was Elmo's perception of his circumstances. He spoke to me from the position of a victim, as if life had foisted these burdens on his shoulders *after* he enrolled in the class. To hear him tell his story, it was somebody else who gave him a full-time job, enrolled him in multiple classes, and then fathered three kids for him to feed, clothe, and tend. Apparently unaware of the part he played in creating his predicament, he felt justified in putting me on notice about all this. He ended our conversation by asking for leniency from me, the professor who would grade him! He made no effort to hide his annoyance when I asked him how many children he had when he registered for the class.

Had Elmo been more self-aware, he'd have covered his bases. He'd make a backup childcare plan in case of babysitter problems; he'd give himself a more forgiving schedule, perhaps taking only one class instead of three.

Elmo is a classic example of someone who lives in a house with no mirrors. These individuals can't recognize themselves as the architect of their problems; they always must be the innocent victim of circumstances brought on by other people. They never find themselves responsible for poor performances or bad outcomes, failed family relationships and lost friends. They know that no matter what goes awry, it has nothing to do with them. This is why so many people don't grow or change. Victims may get by, but they'll never truly enjoy their lives. How could they? Everyone else is spoiling their fun. People with this mindset won't take back their personal power until they understand this concept.

THE BIG PICTURE

Few individuals have severe *Excusitis*, meaning that their houses are 100% mirror free; however, most of us suffer from the condition in some degree. If it were a real disease, doctors would diagnose most people as "mild to moderate"—mirrors in some rooms but not in others. We might take responsibility for our health, for example, but believe that we'll never have a really good job. Or perhaps we micromanage our career, but deep down we believe it's the wrong path and feel stuck in the business we chose twenty years ago. We may even daydream about change and a fuller life, but never act on our ideas. There's always a cargo ship full of reasons why we can't change.

When a person behaves in a powerless, victim-oriented way 100% of the time, examples of excuses and blame are obvious. However, for those of us in the mild-to-moderate range of *Excusitis*, self-defeating justifications can sound deceptively reasonable. Say you're a high school teacher who dreams of owning an ice cream shop. Why aren't you pursuing your dream, or why have you given it up? Here's a list of "frequently cited" reasons why certain aspirations are impossible:

- I can't take that kind of risk while the kids are in college (or preschool or middle school or high school).
- The economy is really bad.
- I have good health insurance at my job, so I'm stuck here.
- We have an obesity epidemic, and my shop would contribute to it.
- Teaching has value, and I help kids and communities. (Some would say ice cream does, too.)

It's important to be realistic when considering such points. But these excuses are also very easy to hide behind. In his book, *Excuses Be Gone! How to Change Lifelong, Self-Defeating Thinking Habits,* psychologist and "motivator-in-chief" Dr. Wayne Dyer explores the power of excuses. He defines them as "mental viruses limiting what we can do."

Our excuses tell us that it's okay if we fail to achieve what we set out to do today. We can always do it tomorrow—maybe—as long as nothing prevents us. Excuses, then, are the default, the norm, the fallback position. Dyer encourages us to examine and eliminate this kind of thinking.

What a great system! We do whatever we want in one area of life or another. So far, so good. If the result is dreadful, we can blame it on circumstances or other people. We don't have to take responsibility because we have our fallback position at the ready.

What happens if we're really successful and we get our dream? That ice cream shop is up and running—great! But some people, to their detriment, may attribute their success to luck:
- It was nothing; I was in the right place at the right time.
- I had luck on my side.
- I finally caught a break.
- Don't cheer yet; my luck won't hold. (The perfect fallback position.)

Rarely do folks say out loud that they worked hard, prepared for a contingency, or took a calculated risk. Perhaps they don't want to brag or seem stuck-up and superior, so they deflect the good outcome away from their sphere of responsibility. It's like how some people will deflect a compliment by negating it.

Dyer uses a quote by Sir Francis Bacon, *"never complain, never explain,"* to explain how excuses can limit and slow our personal growth. When we *complain,* Dyer says, we place blame on someone or something for our problems. When we *explain* ourselves, we often get drawn into arguments about our actions and beliefs—and then make up excuses to defend ourselves. Attributing a good outcome to luck is a form of explaining. We deflect things away from the one responsible. (This is similar to Elmo's attitude that his classes and children "happened to him.") Good results just happen randomly. Although this rationale can provide temporary relief from bad outcomes, it leads to a continuous cycle that impedes personal growth.

Some excuses are obvious, especially when they involve pointing blame at others. Some point to external conditions, such as market conditions or family constraints. But Dyer exposes a different, subtler set of conditions that reflect our inner fears, learned attitudes, and behavior.

Read carefully, and see if you use these kinds of excuses on yourself or others.

The project or goal that I'm about to pursue:
- Is too difficult
- Is too risky
- Will take a long time
- Will raise a ruckus in the family
- Is too big
- Goes against what's been done before

And besides, I'm too old, weak, stupid—and on and on. The biggest *unspoken* excuse of all is: *I don't deserve it!*

Dyer gives us ways to turn those thoughts around and convert them into positive statements. A strong personality, with plenty of personal power, will look at these concerns and say, "So what?" A goal may be difficult or time-consuming, but that doesn't mean you shouldn't try. For many centuries, men and women have accomplished incredible things because their needs or passions led them to persevere. Going to the moon was not an easy undertaking, the first open heart surgery was risky, and composing symphonies or writing poems requires doing something that has never been done before.

Except for obvious exceptions, disparaging self-talk is just another way to bow out of a challenge. Sure, if my dream is to play shortstop for the Cleveland Indians, I may have to hope for another lifetime. But if my goal is to learn French, then I'm still in the game. I'm not too stupid, old, or weak—and neither are you.

Once we face our excuses, we can take our personal power back from them. Dyer offers the following suggestions to help us eliminate the mindsets behind so many common excuses:

➢ REMOVE ALL LABELS

When we define ourselves in a word or two, we place artificial limits on what we can achieve. For example, when we describe ourselves as fat, we provide an excuse for not losing weight. If we say that something is too hard and not worth trying, then we say that we're incapable of doing difficult things.

➢ CONVERSE WITH YOUR UNCONSCIOUS MIND

Statements such as "That's just the way I am," or "That's how I was raised," assume that we lack the power to control our behavior. Be attentive to your inner self-talk. We shape the quality of our lives through what we say to ourselves.

➢ PRACTICE MINDFULNESS

We move toward that upon which we focus. If we chastise ourselves for being overweight, we give our power to the extra pounds and we'll have a harder time losing weight. If we tell ourselves we can't keep track of our car keys, we have a perfect excuse for forgetfulness.

Practicing mindfulness requires that we keep our conscious mind focused on where we are and what we're doing at any given moment. It's surprising how mindfulness makes forgetfulness disappear. The practice of mindfulness is an important step in taking back our personal power.

➤ COMMIT TO OVERCOMING INERTIA

Our excuses tell us it's okay to play it safe. Overcoming inertia often involves taking a risk or trying something new and difficult. Without new challenges, we stagnate, get stuck in familiar ruts, and—before you know it—stop growing.

➤ HARNESS THE POWER OF AFFIRMATIONS

Since our thoughts shape what we become, our excuses thwart our belief in ourselves. We stop believing that we can succeed at anything new or different. *Excusitis* thrives in such a mindset because our brains will then automatically manufacture data to support our failures. We'll always have a litany of excuses to fall back on. "See? I knew I wasn't smart enough or young enough to run a business, raise orchids, or learn to sail." And on it goes.

➤ LIVE IN A SUPPORTIVE UNIVERSE

An unfriendly world is the perfect environment for *Excusitis* to grow; something or someone will always keep us from exploring our deepest desires, no matter what they are. On the other hand, if we see the universe as a friendly place, we can remove the fears and negative obstacles of our own making.

Objective reality is neutral, and our focus is within our control. Think of it this way: In our world, there are just as many good things as bad things. We have control over of the focal point of our attention. It may not seem like it right now, but it's as easy to focus on good things as on bad things. Try finding the positives in your life. You'll notice people responding to you in a different, more upbeat way.

THE CURE FOR *EXCUSITIS*

Armed with this information, you can diagnose your own degree of *Excusitis* by examining a particular instance in your life, perhaps a disappointment or a time you came up short. The steps below will help you gain clarity and, in the future, eliminate excuses from your life.

ASSESS YOUR CURRENT SITUATION

- Where are you now? What is the state of the problem?
- What decisions have you made that created the situation?
- Was another individual influential in your decision?
- What were your expectations regarding this situation?

REVIEW ALL OF THE ACTIONS AND DECISIONS THAT GOT YOU THERE

- Have you said that a problem is because "somebody else talked you into it?" If so, you still hold the ultimate responsibility, not the other person.
- If you made a decision because you were afraid someone would get angry, remind yourself that avoiding confrontation drains your personal power. And, by the way . . .
- Where is this unsolicited dispenser of advice now that you're in a mess?

DECIDE WHAT YOU'LL DO THE NEXT TIME A SITUATION LIKE THIS OCCURS

- Do what you know is best for you, without complaint or explanation.
- Take care of yourself, and let others worry about themselves.

PRACTICE, PRACTICE, PRACTICE

- Take time to think about the ideas and principles in this chapter, and see if you can identify places you can take back your power. This means eliminating excuses.
- Remember that we change our behavior not because we are wrong, but because what we're doing isn't working.
- When you change your behavior, it shows that you've learned and reinforced your ability to take back your power and grow.

If you can grasp the value of taking responsibility—for decisions that turn out poorly along with those that turn out well—you'll have gone a long way toward "healing" your *Excusitis* and gaining mastery over your personal power. This, in turn, is part of developing *emotional intelligence,* the subject of the next chapter.

6

EMOTIONAL INTELLIGENCE, SELF-AWARENESS, AND "BLIND SPOTS"

> *It is very important to understand that Emotional Intelligence is not the opposite of intelligence; it is not the triumph of one's heart over his head. It is the unique intersection of both.*
> — DAVID CARUSO

Feelings are important, and the principles of emotional intelligence (EI) provide us with a context to discuss issues that involve emotions. EI is relatively new as a psychological concept, but it's actually as old as humankind. Our knowledge of it allows us to look at human behavior from a different perspective and gives us a better understanding of why all of us do what we do.

EI was introduced by the 1995 release of *Emotional Intelligence*, a book by psychologist Daniel Goleman. Goleman argued that traditional measures of intelligence—such as the Intelligence Quotient (IQ), which measures cognitive abilities—are too narrow and don't consider interpersonal competence or self-awareness. Goleman broadly defines EI as including *"abilities such as being able to motivate oneself and persist in the face of frustration; to control impulse and delay gratification; to regulate one's moods and keep distress from swamping the ability to think; to empathize and hope."*

I witnessed a great example of EI—or lack thereof—a few years ago when I ran into Brian Smith, one of my high school classmates. He was still quite good-looking, which was how I remembered him. I also recalled him being a brilliant student, and, though a bit shy, he was well liked by everyone in our class. He was our class valedictorian as well as a member of the Phi Beta Kappa Society, an academic honor society of outstanding students in the arts and sciences. We always joked that Brian's IQ was much too high to register on any measurement scale.

In his speech at our commencement ceremony, full of hope and promise, he stated that he wanted to make great positive changes in our world. All the parents in the audience that night probably wished that Brian was their kid. Oh well, there was only one Brian—and then there were the rest of us. We were nice folks, but just didn't display the same promise that he did. I was sure he was going to find a cure for cancer or help create world peace. You know what I mean: the sky was the limit for him. This guy was going places.

Imagine my surprise when he told me that after finishing college, things never worked out for him. He tried many different jobs, but never found the "right fit." He said that his bosses didn't like him (at least that was his perception), and that other people always got the promotions he thought he deserved. He became depressed, his marriage fell apart, and he moved in with his mother. (Usually when one reaches our age, our parents come live with us, not the other way around.) Brian worked part-time in a local repair shop—a fine job, but a far cry from finding a cure for cancer or creating world peace. What the heck happened to this guy?

This is where our knowledge of EI enters the picture. Brian explained his disappointments by focusing on everybody and everything except himself. He made no reference to the role he played in his own life. And he had no ideas for how he could improve his situation. Instead, he focused on his disappointment, on "how his life had turned out." Not once during our conversation did Brian admit his part in creating this mess; there was always something or somebody else to blame. *Excusitis* everywhere!

I wanted to ask Brian why he thought this way, but I decided not to. I was sure he wouldn't want to hear about WYDIWYG and my newly registered trademark. I certainly didn't tell him I was busy writing a book. He probably would've attributed my success to luck anyhow; he told me that the "gods" had turned against him and there was nothing he could do. Brian had little self-awareness of the decisions he made in his life. He had a very low-level EI.

Goleman argues that those with a high level of EI are more likely to have insight into how and why they feel as they do. If Brian had truly examined himself, he would've been more aware of his internal emotions and how they affect his external behavior. He would've been better prepared to face life's trials and tribulations. Instead, Brian gave his power away, accepted the "poor me" way of thinking, and acted as though dark clouds were following him everywhere he went. A higher level of EI—which includes increased self-awareness—would have given Brian the ability to better handle himself and his emotions. He would have had a better life.

In today's workforce, we are judged not only by our intelligence and expertise but also by how we deal with the work environment and relate to each other—whether as managers, team members, or employees. Businesses and organizations want to hire intelligent, highly skilled, and resourceful workers, especially when hiring managers and supervisors.

We all know "book-smart" people who are brilliant at what they do, but lack social skills. They might be mild and introverted, hiding in their offices—or they might be verbally abusive to employees and coworkers. These types are sometimes considered either eccentric or boorish, depending who's doing the talking. We often use strong—even cruel—descriptive phrases for those who are unable to relate meaningfully with others. ("Emotionally crippled" or "emotionally stunted" come to mind.) However, these extreme examples only begin to help us understand the big picture of emotional intelligence.

Let's say that a man has spent a lifetime climbing the corporate ladder. He's a strategic thinker and a great negotiator with terrific communication skills; many people like and admire him. Then, boom—a scandal breaks. He cheated on his income taxes, or his wife—or both! Maybe, in a moment of weakness, he covered up a white-collar crime. All of a sudden, he doesn't look like such a great guy anymore. If he's a public figure, the whole country watches him tumble from power.

If he's truly asked why he did these things, he won't have a ready answer. It could've been poor impulse control or selfishness or—most likely—a blind spot that brought him down. Or perhaps he'd lived in a cocoon of protection and saw himself as above the rules that apply to everyone else. It's clear, however, that this once-powerful person lacked the ability to manage his behavior and emotions. For one reason or another, he mismanaged his personal power, giving it away when it mattered most. He denied the reality staring him in the face.

Hopefully our emotional intelligence won't be exposed to the whole world, but those around us form opinions based on what they can observe: our behavior. Until Daniel Goleman introduced emotional intelligence, we seldom considered that—just like our intellectual abilities—EI is something we can improve with practice.

THE COMPLETE PERSON

EI can also be viewed as "heart intelligence," or EQ: *e*motion *q*uotient. Together with the intellect, which we associate with the brain, we need EQ to become a complete person. According to Jeanne Segal, in her book, *Raising Your Emotional Intelligence*, EQ is ". . . deliberately reminiscent of the standard measure of brainpower, IQ. IQ and EQ are synergistic resources: without one the other is incomplete and ineffectual."

IQ without EQ can get us an "A" on an exam and could even help us land a good job. However, IQ alone is limited; over the long run, without EQ we won't get ahead in any area of life. The quality of our relationships rests in EQ's domain. If our EQ is high, we fully experience our feelings as they happen. A high EQ helps us to identify our beliefs and attitudes through our feelings. And the better we understand ourselves, the higher our EQ. The self-knowledge that goes along with a highly-developed EQ provides a critical edge in work, family, and social settings.

At one time, psychologists believed that we're born with a particular IQ and that, for the most part, it's unchangeable.

They thought that if you were born with an IQ of 115, you'd have that same IQ for the rest of your life. Nowadays, however, these old models of intelligence testing have been found to be inexact. Research suggests that early neurostimulation can influence intelligence and may enhance overall cognitive abilities in early childhood and throughout life.

Emotional intelligence, however, is like a muscle: it strengthens with use. If we don't recognize the importance of EI, we meander through life wearing an emotional blindfold; we'll rarely evaluate our feelings and behavior. On the other hand, if we do recognize the importance of EI, we'll see the value of curiosity about ourselves. We'll learn to observe ourselves, the things we feel and do. And in doing so, we'll strengthen our EQ.

> *Emotional intelligence includes factors such as self-awareness, self-discipline, and empathy, which add up to a different way of being smart.*
> – Daniel Goleman, Ph.D.

EI is the ability to manage ourselves and our relationships in mature and constructive ways. It's also a critical component in self-awareness, which in turn is crucial to recognizing and holding onto our personal power.

Paradoxically, most of us learn from a young age that the intellect is our most important capacity. We place great value on being "smart." Parents tell their kids: "Use your head," or "Use the brain you were born with." Be rational and sensible, we're told. As for feelings—well, they're a bit suspect. We can get into all kinds of trouble with our feelings, can't we? Although we are told that we should value the head and devalue the heart, instinctively, we place great value on our feelings—although we may feel guilty for doing so. (The intellect likes to feel superior.)

From a business perspective, managers and business owners want employees with highly-developed *social* awareness, which they believe leads to a more productive and cooperative workplace. Effective team-building requires members with social awareness. While trends in management come and go, most experts still consider collaborative work and team-building to be worthy pursuits. But let's not put the cart before the horse. To be good collaborators and team members, we first need self-awareness.

We bring who we are to every situation and encounter. To fully develop our social awareness, we need to begin with *self*-awareness. The first step in raising our EQ is to take a look inside and see what's there—and there's always plenty going on. It's worth the time and effort to examine our internal processes using the concepts of EI and EQ. This way, we'll strengthen our self-awareness.

You'll be rewarded for your efforts. As you become more self-aware, you'll:

- Be more effective in your personal and work life;
- Better understand what you're feeling and why;
- Be better able to participate consciously in what you feel and how you respond, rather than just reacting in the same old patterns of the past;

- Be closer and more open with friends you have now—and develop deeper new relationships;
- Be able to better monitor and motivate your progress toward your goals.

So, even before you step foot in your workplace, heightened self-awareness will enrich your internal life and day-to-day interactions.

SELF-AWARENESS, EMOTIONS, AND PERSONAL POWER

My friend Marianne agreed to watch her neighbor Geraldine's house while she was away on an extended trip. Marianne took in the mail, watered the plants, and even made sure the snow was shoveled in front of the house. But for all Marianne's trouble, Geraldine said only a perfunctory "thank you" after she returned to pick up her mail. No chatting about the trip, no time for a cup of coffee. The neighbor took the shopping of bag of mail and left. Marianne didn't hear from her again.

Marianne hadn't wanted anything in particular in return for the favor, but she was surprised that Geraldine didn't try to show her appreciation. A dinner invitation to chat about the trip? A phone call? "Oh, Marianne, I'm so pleased that the plants are alive and well!" Nothing. Marianne went from feeling hurt to feeling angry—and back and forth a few times. And no matter how much she tried to talk herself out of it, Marianne couldn't shake the bad feeling in her heart.

Marianne spent an inordinate amount of time dissecting what had happened—analyzing every point—trying to figure out what was going on. She gave away her power to an event that was over and done with. Marianne is an intelligent person, and she has well-developed EI. But my friend was bothered by being so bothered by Geraldine's actions (or lack thereof). What was going on?

After hearing Marianne's story, I asked her what it was really about. Doesn't the story say more about Geraldine than Marianne? My friend was only hurt because she kept rehashing the event in her mind. Nothing material was lost, so this was clearly an emotional issue. But she hadn't resented watching her neighbor's house in the least. Marianne finally realized that it was Geraldine's lack of acknowledgment. It came as a surprise. Her neighbor's behavior seemed out of character, although Marianne admitted she knew Geraldine only as a neighbor.

To help her look at the situation from another angle, I presented Marianne with some hypothetical scenarios. What if something horrible happened on Geraldine's trip? What if she had to deal with a family crisis the minute she got home? Would that change Marianne's feelings? "Well, yes," Marianne said, "that *would* make a difference."

On the other hand, what if Geraldine was an indifferent person? Not overtly rude in day-to-day interactions, but thoughtless about relationships and inconsiderate of other people's feelings? Would Marianne take it personally then? No, she probably wouldn't.

Marianne's issue is really with herself. The neighbor is only a bit player in the story; what matters most is Marianne's self-awareness. My friend had tied herself into knots when she only had incomplete information. She didn't know if this was Geraldine's typical behavior or if these were special circumstances. But, oh, how it seemed to matter.

This story led me to discover one essential truth about human behavior: *We're all normal.* I can see your reaction.

What about your crazy Uncle Bill? Or that impossible woman you work for? Are they really normal? My thesis is they are, because no matter what anyone does, there's a reason for it.

We rarely know the reason for a person's behavior; in fact, most of the time we have no idea why people act as they do. Nobody has that degree of personal intuition. That's why it's most important to be aware of ourselves, our behavior, and our reactions to others. One of the powers that EI gives us is the ability to look inside and monitor our own feelings and reactions. Ultimately, Marianne recognized that she gave away her power over a perceived slight for no obvious reason.

MARIANNE'S LESSON

Marianne's frustrating experience with Geraldine taught her just how little she could know about another person's intentions. She also learned that her unhappiness didn't come from the outside—from Geraldine—but rather that it came from within. She gave away her power to a person she barely knew, over behavior she didn't understand and couldn't explain.

Marianne's experience is common. We react to things so quickly that we begin to think that the external world can be fully understood: this person makes us feel a certain way; that person is wrong for treating us so badly. In these situations, we give away our power. Why? We are unconscious of what we're doing. This is a sign that we need to develop our self-awareness, which is a vital component of emotional intelligence.

How we experience life—and other people—is 100% dependent on our awareness of who we are. It's always an inside job. Once we understand this principle, we are far more likely to effectively manage our personal power.

WHAT HOLDS US BACK FROM SELF-AWARENESS?

If you sometimes think that life is passing you by, you're right—but in a different way than the phrase implies. Today's fast-paced living keeps us focused on to-do lists, deadlines, catching the next train, finding parking places, or deciding what to throw together for dinner. While we're hard at work at our desks, our minds flit about—thinking about the kids in day care, the dog at home, or the unfinished report due in two weeks. With so many distractions around, too often we focus on the next thing to be done, rather than on what we're doing in the moment.

Meanwhile, where do our emotions hang out? Oh, our feelings haven't gone anywhere. They're always with us, but we usually ignore them. We're only aware of them when they build up and boil over.

Once we practice and develop self-awareness, we can understand and appreciate our emotions and acknowledge their influence in our lives. Emotions don't only have a once-in-a-while influence; rather, their influence is ongoing—whether or not we enjoy any given emotional experience.

Emotions, which we also call feelings, are reactions to important events or thoughts. They can be pleasant or unpleasant in varying degrees. According to Goleman, emotions that "simmer beneath the threshold of awareness can have a powerful impact on how we perceive and react, even though we have no idea they are at work."

Self-aware or not, we act according to the way we feel, and we're completely accountable for our behavior. Self-aware individuals with developed EI take responsibility for their actions and their consequences. Of course, no one is perfect. My friend Marianne usually handles her emotions in a highly developed and enlightened way. But the situation with Geraldine surprised her and took her off her game, which led her to look outside of herself rather than keeping her focus inside.

What is an external focus? Unfortunately, most of us have been trained from childhood to look outside of ourselves to fix, control, or change the people who we believe cause us internal discomfort. Most of us are long on lamenting:

- "Look what you made me do!"
- "If you'd just listened to me, I could . . ."
- "You're the cause of this problem."
- "Don't you see that this entire mess is your fault?"
- "He started it!"

All these statements are an attempt to alleviate the burden of an unpleasant situation. If only things around us were different, life would be better—or so we like to think. We give away our power every time we blame someone.

The statements above show us the opposite of EI. Most of us were taught to deal with frustration by pointing away from ourselves and to someone else. Sometimes, it's not a person we point to, but an institution: the government, the legal system, the car dealership, our kids' school. Any large, unaccountable system will do.

Unfortunately, an external focus provides little if any resolution to the vicissitudes of life and frequently leads to frustration and interpersonal conflict. By the time we reach adulthood, we have a tremendous amount of buried pain. We then share "what we know" with our children, thereby perpetuating the cycle and burying our negative feelings deep within. As children grow to adulthood, they continue to look for external sources on which to blame their unhappiness.

As this continues, our emotional pain is ignored and buried—until it erupts.

Know thyself. – Socrates

As we work on our self-awareness, we uncover and marvel at what truly makes each of us unique and precious. This is what personal growth is about. Once begun, this journey offers new hope because it exposes us to fresh ideas about life and getting along with others. Recognizing our emotions, coupled with enlightened self-awareness, accelerates our growth and healing and helps us reach our potential.

SELF-ASSESSMENT LEADS TO SELF-AWARENESS

Self-assessment is the cornerstone of self-awareness. It helps us understand emotions and EI, and it allows us to evaluate our strengths, limitations, values, and motives. It builds intimacy with our own inner resources and abilities.

Competent self-assessment requires a candid view of our behavior and the vigilance to discover "blind spots" in our observations.

I DIDN'T SEE IT, SO IT CAN'T BE SO

Blind spots—also known as selective perception—alter our reality and can cause us great pain and loss of personal power. We usually see what we want to see and ignore information that might lead us to make a different decision. Most of us understand selective perception when it comes to *others*, but it's challenging to accurately identify it in ourselves because we "trust" what we see. How many times have you said, "Don't tell me I'm wrong, I saw it with my own eyes?" We believe that our perceptions are always accurate and correct.

Sadly, when told we need to change our behavior, many of us interpret this as a sign of failure, weakness, or just being wrong. Because of our fear of losing face and the pain that comes with altering our self-image, we may deny the need to change.

Perceived deficiencies in our behavior are a "bitter cup of tea to swallow." Our unexamined core beliefs will tell us that what we are already doing is right. Thus, our idea of what "should be" often leads us to deny reality.

Goleman defines denial as an "emotionally uncomfortable strategy that protects us from the distress that acknowledging the harsh truth would bring." In other words, we'd rather avoid the short-term stress of change than reap the long-term gains of self-awareness.

When someone consistently mishandles certain situations, it's a sure sign that they're in denial. For example, a person declares bankruptcy once, but feels like a victim after she falls into debt again. Or someone loses one job after another because he doesn't show up on time, but always manages to blame his boss.

If we dismiss problems as bad luck or blame someone else for them, self-awareness vanishes and denial stays in the driver's seat. We find fault with other people and never question ourselves, which constantly reinforces our own blind spots. We mentally edit actual events and delude ourselves about everyone else's culpability, all the while letting our personal power drain away. At this point, we aren't even aware of our personal power. We solidify the conviction that our problems—or "bad luck"—are always because of what someone else did. Isn't life unfair?

This behavior leads us to insist that we're innocent in every way. I didn't get invited to the party because "they're all stuck up." I'm not included in the group because "they're jealous of me."

Robert Kaplan, formerly of the Center for Creative Leadership, conducted a study about blind spots. His research provides a helpful list of some of the more common—and costly—ones:

Blind ambition: These individuals must win or appear "right" at all costs. They don't cooperate; they compete, and they're good at exaggerating their value and contribution. Boastful and arrogant, they see people in black-and-white terms and categorize everyone as an ally or enemy.

Unrealistic goals: These men and women set overly ambitious, unattainable goals for themselves and others. They're unrealistic about what it takes to get things done.

Relentless striving: These people are vulnerable to burnout because they work compulsively at the expense of all else in life. Eventually, they're running on "empty."

Drives others: Prone to pushing other people too hard, these individuals end up watching others burn out. They have high expectations of other people, but come across as abrasive or ruthless and insensitive. They're oblivious to the emotional harm they inflict on others.

Power hungry: They seek power for their own interests, generally pushing a personal agenda without regard for other perspectives. Others see them as exploitative.

Insatiable need for recognition: Addicted to glory, these people take credit for others' efforts and blame them for mistakes. Always looking ahead, they sacrifice follow-through in pursuit of the next victory.

Preoccupation with appearance: These individuals need to look good at all costs and are preoccupied with public image. Along with appearance, they crave the material trappings of prestige.

Need to seem perfect: Enraged by or rejecting criticism—even realistic, helpful criticism—these people blame others for their failures and are unable to admit mistakes or personal weaknesses.

Clearly, blind spots can motivate people to *avoid* self-awareness. After all, if we know ourselves, then we can admit our failings. But, if we can't bear to acknowledge our blind spots, we remain in denial. This is truly sad, because all behavior is learned; if we're deficient in one area and acknowledge the problem, we can learn to improve.

Arrogant or impatient people can *learn* to listen and respect others' views. Workaholics can slow down and find more balance in life. Even ruthless people can change and see the harm they've done. In all these cases, emotional intelligence can be developed and enhanced. However, to improve and change, we need to take a first step, and that involves becoming aware of how these habits damage us, poison our relationships, and rob us of our personal power.

BEGIN YOUR SELF-ASSESSMENT

To improve your self-awareness and raise the level of your EI, I suggest you slow down and engage in some self-analysis. Take a sincere look at yourself. If you're focused on a problem that you perceive as external, move to an *in*ternal focus. Ask yourself:

- What am I feeling right now, and where's my focus?
- Do I always have to be right?
- What message is my body language sending?
- How do others react to me?

The goal is to genuinely observe your behavior, not find reasons for it. If you find that your "mind chatter" is making excuses for your actions and is busy judging the behavior of others, then you're not doing *self*-assessment. This takes you away from self-awareness and puts you back into long-standing behavior patterns—and denial.

You can come back to this exercise whenever you find yourself reacting or going down an unhelpful train of thought. In addition, observe other people and ask for their impressions. *Emotionally intelligent people intentionally seek feedback.* Self-aware individuals want to hear how others perceive them because it's valid information they can use for self-evaluation.

Honest evaluation doesn't offend emotionally intelligent people, and they don't lose personal power when they're challenged to become more self-aware. They direct their energy toward self-analysis, with the goal of developing more pleasant, inviting, and productive behavior. This leads them toward their goals and a richer internal life.

So, go ahead, raise your EQ!

7

WHAT'S MY PART IN THIS DRAMA?

> *Only you can hold yourself back, only you can stand in your own way. Only you can help yourself.*
> — **Mikhail Strabo**

Day in and day out, situations arise in which we must take action. We may need to talk with another person about a problem, or perhaps something prompts us to reexamine a long-held attitude or belief. The choices we make, both big and small, form the foundation on which we build our lives, and our decisions guide our experiences.

We can't always control what comes our way, but we can control how we respond. For example, we choose what time to set our alarm; if we're perpetually late, what part are we playing in the stressful drama that follows? Is there a flaw in our plan? If our coworker turns up the air conditioning in the office every day and we're freezing to death, what's our role? Where can we exercise choice?

The first example seems like a no-brainer, but you'd be surprised by how many people look outside of themselves for ways to justify being late. They throw up their hands as if helpless in the face of outside forces. It's the bus schedule or the rush-hour traffic; the kids are always pokey about getting ready for school. They'll look everywhere but within themselves. This reflects a lack of self-awareness; most likely, these folks have a ready excuse for every problem, mistake, or obstacle they encounter.

Maggie, an acquaintance of mine, felt helpless and victimized on a daily basis. For two years, her coworker, Gerry, had been cranking up the air conditioning, causing her and several others to keep wool blazers handy in the middle of July. The temperature in the office was well below what ordinary people find comfortable. Maggie and her colleagues took the attitude that Gerry *made* them pile on extra clothes.

This situation is trickier than changing a pattern you can directly control, such as leaving the house earlier to get to work on time. Yes, emotional maturity and self-awareness are needed to change personal behavior, but solving interpersonal problems calls on these traits even more. When people approach me with this type of dilemma, my first question always is, "What part do *you* play in the situation?"

More often than not, they shake their heads and defensively say, "Nothing. I don't have a part in this. I'm not the one turning up the air conditioner. What can I do?" That was Maggie's reply. She didn't like it when I said, "We *always* have a part in these dramas."

Maggie and her coworkers had given away their power for two years. They griped to each other, making exaggerated gestures and sarcastic remarks as they donned their blazers—sometimes mockingly pulling on winter hats. One would think Gerry would take the hint, but most of us have an astounding ability to ignore "hints." With every gripe session and sarcastic gesture, their personal power drained away, just as surely as water swirls down a bathtub drain.

I asked Maggie why she hadn't spoken up for such a long time. She and the others could have simply gone to him and said, "We need to compromise on the office temperature. Most of the time, we have to take extreme measures to stay warm."

Maggie and her coworkers made the mistake of *not* stating the obvious. They expected Gerry to read their minds, interpret their sarcasm, and logically conclude that he needed to adjust to a warmer temperature. Because he didn't, Maggie and colleagues assumed he was just an insensitive dunderhead.

As Maggie and I talked, I kept bringing it back to her part in the office drama. She had gone along with the others and wasted two years griping instead of acting. Still, she was reluctant to admit her role in the "Great Freezing Office Caper." Somehow, she still believed her coworker should've known better and that the cold office was entirely his fault—100%.

After our conversation, Maggie approached her coworkers to formulate a plan to change the temperature—and social dynamic—of the office. Eventually, they approached Gerry and told him they'd been uncomfortable with the temperature in the office for a long time. Predictably, he said, "Really? Why didn't you say something before now?"

As the spokesperson, Maggie explained that they'd tried to show him in all kinds of ways that they were freezing.

He looked puzzled. Maggie realized that the man hadn't put two and two together. He never paid enough attention to note their sarcasm. Only when they explained that they were forced to wear extra layers did Gerry get it. He didn't like the warmer temperature, but he began working in his shirtsleeves, and the others in the office were satisfied. Still, it took a few weeks to transform and repair the atmosphere in the office.

It's clear that Maggie and her colleagues could have handled the situation in short order. Rather than doing that, however, they assumed the role of victims and claimed there was nothing they could do. By not standing up for themselves, they gave away their power. It was easier for them to blame Gerry, so eventually the conflict developed into a harmful feedback loop. For his own part, Gerry demonstrated that he lacked awareness and had no idea how others perceived him.

> Be who you are and say what you feel, because those who mind don't matter and those who matter don't mind.
> – Dr. Seuss (Theodore Seuss Geisel)

THE LANGUAGE OF "YOU MADE ME . . ."

Each of us creates our own life experience. This is the basic premise of self-awareness. Except in extreme situations of oppression and abuse, in our society no one can physically *force* us do anything once we reach adulthood and independence. However, our language doesn't always reflect this. Who hasn't heard (or been) a parent who shouts, "You better pick up those toys. . . . Don't make me come in there and give you spanking." If the parent loses patience and spanks the child, he or she may say, "Look what you made me do."

If we believe that someone *makes* us do anything, we have a personal power deficit. In those moments, we lack self-awareness. And in extremely stressful situations, our bodies and minds can become emotionally hijacked. "Emotional hijacking" is when the rational, decision-making part of the brain is temporarily taken over by the amygdala, a more primitive part of the brain that reacts with raw emotion. However, we can learn to make choices and take responsibility for our actions even in times of high stress.

Just to be clear, no one can ever make us:

- Yell, scream, or strike at another person;
- Speed down the highway (even if we're late or if another driver makes us angry);
- Work for a specific salary or for a tyrannical boss—we may feel stuck for a variety of reasons, but we can plan for a change in the future;
- Buy a house we can barely afford;
- Drink too much or take illegal drugs—or pour money into a slot machine;
- Spend outside our means on clothing or jewelry;
- Cheat on our taxes or on a test;
- Gossip or otherwise speak poorly about another person or group of people;
- Eat more than we know is good for us;

- Do a favor for another person—we can choose to do favors, but no can make us;
- Attend every family event—from Thanksgiving to Passover or Easter or Ramadan.

You get the picture!

VICTIMS NO MORE

You may have heard of Mika Brzezinski, the co-host of "Morning Joe," a popular morning news and commentary show on MSNBC. She's also the author of *Knowing Your Value: Women, Money and Getting What You're Worth*. In her book, she describes how she felt when she realized that she made significantly less money than her co-host, Joe Scarborough, a former Congressman turned media commentator. She expected to be paid somewhat less, since the show was designed around Joe as the primary host, while she played the role of "sidekick." But Mika eventually learned that Joe's salary was *fourteen times* hers. And that's not all. Mika realized she was making much less money than many of the paid commentators that appeared on the show.

"Morning Joe" rapidly rose in the ratings, and everyone agreed that Mika was a big part of its success. But when she first asked for a raise, she was turned down. Eventually, Mika decided that she was willing to walk away from the show if she continued to be so grossly undervalued. That was the key, and Mika describes it as a moment of truth. She recognized a pattern in herself that—using our language—led to the loss of her power. Mika explains that she'd acted this way on other jobs, too, which had left her feeling beleaguered and resentful. In Mika's case, knowing her value meant embracing her personal power. Mika saw this pattern in other women's lives as well.

Mika's book became popular in part because so many women identified with her story, but also because it contradicts assumptions most of us have about media figures. They usually look pretty powerful, don't they? Who would've thought Mika worked with such salary disparity?

The story of Mika and Joe encapsulates what goes into personal change and taking your power back. For those who feel undervalued in their workplace or relationships, here are a few guidelines for taking back power:

TAKE THE ISSUE OF "RIGHT AND WRONG" OUT OF THE SITUATION:

When we feel slighted, wallowing in indignation only leads to helplessness and blame. Inevitably, we give a moral overtone to the situation at hand, no matter what it may be. But everyday conflicts involving our personal power are not moral issues. We must ask ourselves: do we want to feel righteous and superior, or do we want to end the day feeling happy? We can go through our days like self-righteous martyrs, but suffering in silence never leads to happiness; on the contrary, it almost always leads to resentment and, eventually, hostility.

Many years ago, as a part of completing a program in nuclear medicine, I was required to serve a one-year internship at a hospital. Most of the hospitals that wanted nuclear medicine students were located outside of Ohio. Since I didn't want to relocate, I was grateful that a small hospital located thirty-five miles from Cleveland selected me. The program also picked Robert M., a fellow student. We were assigned to work together at the hospital, and I was happy about the way things were turning out. I looked forward to working with Robert, a nice guy.

On our very first day, the chief radiologist took me aside and said, "You understand that Robert will make a little more money than you because he is a man." I was shocked and disappointed, but I didn't know what to say; so with a smile on my face and an angry tension in my stomach, I agreed. Today I can't believe I agreed to make this my reality. However, I did just that for a couple of reasons:

1. I didn't want to move to a hospital out of state to complete my program;
2. I was unaware of the existence of the Equal Employment Opportunity Commission (EEOC). (In 1964 the EEOC was formed to prevent discrimination based on gender, color, nationality, and so forth.)

Looking back, even if I'd been aware of my legal rights, I'm not sure I'd have had enough gumption to confront the radiologist about the pay disparity. He had positional as well as referent power—and, in my mind, I had none. What right did I have to question the chief radiologist of the hospital? I was just a student at the only in-state hospital available to me.

Notice how I was in a self-imposed box. I could've recognized my power and refused to work for less money, but there would be a consequence: I'd have to finish the program out of state. Looking back, why I didn't want to make the move is beyond me. I was single, and finishing my education was my sole responsibility. But this was lost on me back then. Things had to be my way or else I'd victimize myself. I played the role of a martyr every day of my life. If I had died back then, my tombstone would've read: "Poor me. It was awful."

Today, with a healthier outlook on life, I realize that not only had I given away all of my power over the pay issue, my refusal to relocate had boxed me in. Of course I couldn't see that at the time. Instead, I was livid with Robert! How dare he get more money than me? I walked around angry and helpless—until I realized that all I was doing was reminding myself of how cheated I felt. So, not only was I earning less than Robert, I also was making myself miserable every day. Everyone else in my version of the scenario was immoral and wrong; that way I could plant my feet on the moral high ground.

But in reality, Robert had nothing to do with the situation. Why the heck was I wasting my energy being hostile to him? The radiologist made the decision, and I went along with it. I'd ruled out all other options. I was going to be at that hospital for a full year. That was the reality. It was up to me to either enjoy my days there or endure them in misery.

Thankfully, after many resentment-filled weeks, I took back my power and made the best of the remaining months of my education. I had many terrific coworkers at the hospital and made some new friends. When I look back at that year, I can see that, overall, I enjoyed myself, had some fun, and learned a great deal.

I use this example from my own life because it illustrates what happens when we miss an opportunity to use our personal power, experience the consequences, and then manage to make the best of it. Did my circumstances change? No, not at all. Was the lower wage unfair? Absolutely. But I eventually took control over what I could, namely, *myself*.

Once I was able to get past my anger, I owned up to the part I played in this drama: I accepted unequal pay for identical work. Exercising my personal power meant taking responsibility for my decision and, perhaps most importantly, not making everybody miserable—including myself—during that year. Yes, the situation was unfair, but I'd agreed to it. The issue of right and wrong was no longer personal. But had I continued working at that hospital, confronting the legal issue of equal pay for equal work would have been the right thing to do.

When I tell this story, I'm sometimes asked about the radiologist—more to the point, I'm asked if I judge him harshly. For all I know, he didn't know about the law, or perhaps his superiors dictated the salaries. Maybe years later he realized the injustice, maybe not. What matters to me are the actions I took and the changes I made to my life.

It's your fault.

It is far easier to blame someone than to take the time to understand them.
– David Gurteen

This experience also taught me that in a business situation, people have some issues in common and some that differ, depending on the self-interest and financial investment of each party. Except in extreme situations (ignoring essential worker safety, for example), these are not moral issues. The parties simply look at a single situation from different angles. This is the lesson Mika Brzezinski learned, and in a different context, it's the lesson Maggie and her colleagues learned, too.

EXAMINE OUR PATTERNS:

The classic definition of insanity is doing the same thing again and again and expecting different results. This assumes, however, that we're aware of the behaviors and patterns we're repeating. If we go through the motions unaware of the role we play in our own life, we'll be doomed to repeat our behavior and experience the same outcomes—and feel just as bad every time. Maybe we take yet another job where the starting salary is well below what we think we deserve. Again we tell ourselves that this is a temporary fix and that in six months things will turn around. A year later, we drag ourselves to a job that we hate, feeling victimized. Until we ask ourselves what our part is in being consistently underpaid, the pattern will go on and we'll continue to lose our personal power. It's not a matter of right or wrong; it's a matter of self-awareness.

SEPARATE OUT WHO OWNS WHAT:

In our earlier example, Maggie and her colleagues had a difficult time admitting their role in the freezing office fiasco. For months they griped instead of taking action, expecting "that jerk" Gerry to change his behavior. Only when they agreed to take responsibility for their part in the drama did a change in the office climate take place. While they weren't responsible for Gerry's behavior, they were responsible for their own silence.

People often tell me about problems they have with family members or neighbors. Paradoxically, I hear one story after another in which these individuals take ownership of other people's problems—but are blind to their own. People aren't responsible for their neighbor's perpetually barking dog. Parents aren't responsible for the money their son needs to pay his half-dozen parking tickets. But people act and feel like they're deeply involved.

Someone might claim they can't call the police about a barking dog because they like the neighbor too much. This is precisely the problem. Because they won't go speak to the neighbor, the dog continues to be an annoyance and bad feelings fester. Eventually, someone in the area will call the police, and a minor issue will blow up into a major dispute.

Likewise, the parents feel roped into taking on the financial burden of their son's mistakes. They play a harmful part by refusing to say no to their young adult son, thereby letting him avoid the consequences of careless parking. At this point, he's being careless with his parents' money, too.

CHANGING OUR BEHAVIOR DOESN'T MEAN WE WERE AT FAULT

Too often, people assume that if they change the way they do things or alter their thinking, it's an admission that they were completely wrong before. But again, owning our power (and taking back power) isn't about right or wrong. It's about self-awareness and action. If we speak to our son about his parking tickets and either refuse to give him the money or write out a contract for repayment, we don't have to chew over our lenient past behavior. We're taking back our power, that's all.

When we change our behavior, it simply means we learned something. On one day, we might take a particular action, but learn that our behavior was unproductive, so we'll change what we do the next time a similar situation arises. That's what my friend Maggie did when she was dissatisfied with her working conditions. Sometimes being fed up with a situation leads us to finally ask ourselves if we have a part in what's going on. Most of us usually don't change unless we're in extreme pain or distress.

When we examine our part in a situation, we're taking responsibility. Rather than going through regret or blame, once we do this we seldom fall back into victim mode again. Lois, an old friend, once told me a story about agreeing to look after a neighbor's cat. Knowing that my friend has a cat dander allergy, I wondered why she'd do such a thing. What was she thinking?

Lois had more to say, though. She thought about what she'd done and admitted to herself that she'd agreed to take care of the cat because she really disliked saying no. If someone asked her for a favor, Lois almost never said no; if her child's school or her church needed a volunteer, they always called Lois. As she thought about the cat curling up on her couch, Lois knew what would happen to her—sneezing, watering eyes, and needing to keep an inhaler handy. Finally, she realized she had to tell her friend she couldn't keep the cat.

What impressed me about Lois's action was her willingness to take responsibility for a mistake. She understood that she never should've agreed to this arrangement. I asked how she'd approached her friend to tell her she'd changed her mind.

"I told her that I'd made a mistake," Lois said, "and once I described my allergic reaction, my friend was very upset with me."

"Really?" I asked.

"She felt terrible that I'd ever agreed to take care of the cat in the first place!"

The situation turned out fine, but Lois said the worst part had been facing the possibility that she'd lose the relatively new friendship. "I would've saved myself a boatload of worry if I'd said no right away and explained why."

This experience served Lois well in a few ways. First, she took back her power and, in doing so, took care of herself and her needs. Second, she owned the problem. Her friend didn't know about the allergy, and Lois realized it wasn't fair to withhold the information. Lois also admitted to feeling physically jittery and anxious when she picked up the phone to call her friend. This case of nerves wasn't a warning that her action was dangerous, but rather it exposed her extreme reluctance to say no. Noting her feelings and overcoming them taught Lois about herself, and it helped her break a pattern and change her behavior in the future.

Lois explained that her mother was the organizer, chairwoman, and president of a long string of organizations and committees. At her mother's knee, Lois learned it was her duty to help out and make her community better. Who can argue with that? The trouble is that Lois had a full-time career as a hospital administrator, whereas Lois's mother was a full-time volunteer. Lois was trying to be both—and the results were awful. Every time she thought about saying no, anxious symptoms appeared in her body. Just think, Lois's path to growth and taking back her personal power started with a cat.

MORE "I," LESS "YOU"

We aren't being self-centered when we use "I statements." In fact, when it comes to owning our responsibilities, it's important that we speak in a way that implies ownership. Here are a few examples of what we sound like when don't own our part in a dispute, and what we sound like when we do:

Blame: *You're always late for dinner, and you insult me and my cooking.*

Own: *I decided to go ahead and eat dinner at six o'clock so I can get on with my evening.*

Blame: *You and your parking tickets have drained my checkbook dry—you're so inconsiderate.*

Own: *I made a decision not to cover your parking ticket fines.*

Blame: (speaking to a third party) *She's the worst boss ever. She makes me hate going to work every day.*

Own: (speaking to a third party) *I've procrastinated about talking to my boss about a department transfer or negotiating with her over working conditions. I intend to stop griping and start acting.*

Simply put, when we blame, we lose power, but when we own our part, we gain power. Of course, we might not solve everything, and there might be consequences down the road. In the first example, the husband or wife chooses to eat alone and then goes on about what remains of the day. It's not ideal, but it's better than trying to keep a hot dinner from getting cold and stewing over their spouse's rude behavior.

And yes, the son who can't follow parking laws might get in a snit because his parents won't bail him out. At some point, the parents need to say, "So what?" Sometimes a snit is necessary to reveal troubled family patterns.

In the third case, the person admits the need to change, even though the exact nature of the change has yet to be determined.

AND NOW THE GOOD NEWS

We might think that owning our part is serious, even stressful. *Oh boy, what do I have to change now? How tough will it be?* However, if we must own the unpleasant parts of our lives, we can take ownership of the good parts, too. Many of us are very good putdown artists—of ourselves—and think we're showing good manners when we deflect accomplishments and attribute good news to luck.

Success is often defined as "preparation meeting opportunity." Notice it's not "preparation meeting luck." Sure, when some good things happen—say, finding the perfect shoes for a wedding or meeting a manager who just happens to be hiring—we might say we were lucky. ("Good fortune" is probably a better term.) Most of the time, however, we developed our skills and put in the hard work first; only then does opportunity come knocking. It feels like luck, but we earned it.

It's neither arrogant nor bad manners to own your part in the good things that happen to you. If you went to night school and earned a degree that led to a promotion, that's not luck: it's a perfect example of preparation meeting opportunity. Maybe you worked hard as the assistant manager for several years, and when the manager retired, you took her place. Is that luck? No, you excelled at your job and were rewarded. If things hadn't worked out, though, you'd be free to take those hard-earned skills and hunt for a better job.

For some, attributing every unpleasant event in their lives to bad luck lets them off the hook—the hand of fate made them lose their jobs, not poor performance. But to retain personal power, you must examine what happened on the job and face unpleasant truths. Well, the same goes for the good things. If you economized in certain areas of your life—perhaps saving money on groceries and clothes or forgoing your favorite coffee drink at Starbucks—and saved the money for a great vacation, then take pleasure in claiming the part you played in making the trip happen.

When you cultivate self-awareness, you're able to stop yourself from blaming or explaining. You also can reverse course and enjoy the fruits your efforts produce in your life.

8

HAVE YOU EVER BEEN HIJACKED?—EMOTIONALLY, THAT IS

> He who controls others might be powerful, but he who has mastered himself is mightier still.
> — Lao-Tzu

Have you ever been so angry that you react—even take action—without thinking? I've never known anyone who has said no to that question. Consider these examples:

- A person—anyone, even a stranger—annoys you so much that you immediately "blow a fuse" and say things you don't mean. You don't even recognize yourself.

- Somebody cuts in front of you in the grocery store line, and you launch into a tirade that has everyone within earshot doubting *your* sanity.
- You yell at the computerized voice menu when trying to solve a problem with your phone bill. When you finally talk to a human being, you take out your frustration on the customer service rep.
- You tell the radio or television to "shut up" when you hear a commentator or a program guest say something you find stupid.
- You're so furious with a family member that you rush from the room, fearful you might say something you can't take back. If you're married, you probably want a divorce; if you're a parent, you're wondering why you had that kid in the first place.
- Feeling victimized by a family member, you *don't* rush from the room and instead fly into a rage, threatening or insulting them. Some folks pride themselves on the ability to "tell people off" or come up with the best wisecrack.
- After a day when everything seemed to go wrong, you shout at other drivers left and right—literally. They come out of nowhere and cut you off, drift too close to your lane, or otherwise upset you.
- Some poor, unsuspecting person is your "last straw." It doesn't matter who it is, but it's the end of a very bad day. You're rude to them in ways you aren't proud of later on.

The above responses tend to be instantaneous. You don't take time to consider the results of your behavior; all you know is that "something" set you off. Frankly, if you're alone in your car and you yell at the radio host, no harm done—although it could be a warning that you're too stressed out. But most of these scenarios represent a true loss of personal power. In the heat of irrational behavior, we lose our self-awareness and our sense of choice and autonomy.

Say you respond to a difficult person by yelling and screaming all kinds of things you really don't mean. When you eventually calm down, you'll invariably wish you hadn't behaved in such an ugly way. Remorse is a reminder that you behaved badly and lost control. Once the damage has been done, however, you must try to repair the mess.

Most of us make solemn promises to get a hold of ourselves and never, never let something like that happen again, no matter how badly we're provoked. We have good intentions, for sure, but the cycle is difficult to break.

Some years ago, I arrived home from work tired after a challenging day, looking forward to a night of quiet solitude. As I walked through the front door, I heard the phone ringing and hurried to pick it up. (Why? No good reason. Without thinking, I responded to the "stimulus" of a ringing phone. Notice how I relinquished my power to the telephone. No law demands that ringing telephones must be immediately answered—and doing so shot my chance for solitude.) The caller was a salesperson eager to sell me aluminum siding. I politely explained that I live in a thirty-story brick building and have no use for aluminum siding. He promptly hung up without a polite thank-you or even a goodbye. I let it annoy me. I forgot that I'm the one in charge of my thoughts and feelings. Notice how I gave my power away by expecting a polite phone call from a stranger?

The Dali Llama says, "expectations are the death of serenity"; thus, it follows that when we place our values and expectations on others, we're often disappointed. Should the caller have been more polite? Of course. Given that, how much more power and emotional investment should I have given that thought? None! I could've taken my power back right away, but it was a rotten day and I was on a roll. I had barely managed to get my coat off before the phone rang again. This time it was a campaign volunteer reminding me to vote on Tuesday. It was the sixth time they'd called, and for the sixth time I explained I'd already cast an absentee ballot. Now I was really annoyed, and I asked if these volunteers ever checked off names or corrected their phone lists.

My "last straw" came when the phone rang a third time. Another salesperson, this one selling windows. I'd had it. "No . . . *thank* . . . *you*," I said through tight jaws before plunking down the receiver. A few minutes later, the phone rang for the fourth time. No more Ms. Nice Woman! Needless to say I was less than gracious, and shouted, "*Now what?!*" into the phone.

Well, it was my elderly aunt calling to see how I was because she hadn't heard from me for a while. Talk about feeling like a total slug! Naturally, I was ashamed and embarrassed. First, why hadn't we stayed in touch? I could've been considerate enough to check in with her. And now, when this lovely woman took the time to call and inquire about me, I greeted her with my nasty attitude. My response was so immediate that I didn't consider the possibility that this fourth call could be anything other than another interruption—my last straw.

THE AMYGDALAE—YOU DON'T LEAVE HOME WITHOUT THEM

You've probably had your share of experiences like the one above and have found yourself apologizing for offensive behavior or insults made in a fit of anger. Daniel Goleman, referred to earlier in our discussion of Emotional Intelligence, called these sudden emotional whirlwinds *amygdala (ah-*mig*'-dah-lah) hijackings.*

The *Amygdala*—the Greek word for "almond"—is a tiny part of the brain that looks like an inch-long almond. (We actually have two amygdalae, one on each side of the brain, but most researchers refer to the "amygdala" [singular] rather than "amygdalae" [plural]. In this book, I'll use the singular form.) Through a series of connections to other centers in the brain, the amygdala forms a critical part of our intricate limbic system: it's the emotional component of the nervous system

Goleman believes that the connections between the amygdala (the "feeling" part of the brain) and related limbic structures (the "thinking" parts of the brain) are the hub of the encounters between head and heart, thought and feeling. The amygdala is the "specialist" for emotional matters: it's the storehouse for emotional memory. Life without it is stripped of personal meaning.

The amygdala processes and stores emotional memory, which is critical to the way we respond, moment to moment, to what goes on around us—and within us. The amygdala matches incoming sensory stimuli with emotional memories, scanning them for threats and allowing us to recognize dangerous situations. In this way, the amygdala occupies a powerful post in mental life; it's the equivalent of a psychological sentinel. In Goleman's words, the amygdala functions like "an alarm company where operators stand ready to send out emergency calls to the fire department, police, and a neighbor whenever a home security system signals trouble."

These alarm signals are sent to your nervous system before the rational part of your brain can decide if the intrusion is legitimate. Yep! Like it or not, we feel before we think. Instantly thrust into behavior, we have no time to reason. Our urge is to either "get away" or to "stay and battle." The fight-or-flight response immediately engages the adrenal glands (and other systems), which feels like tightness in the body or a pounding heart. The more intense the response, the less likely it is that logic and reason become involved.

I'm reminded of a young neighborhood girl who was attacked by a pit bull a few years ago. After a trip to an emergency room and thirty-one stitches in her head and neck, she recovered, physically. But my guess is that, for the rest of her life, the sight of an approaching dog will trigger an emotional reaction, leading her to feelings of fear and a desperate need to escape. In this situation, her amygdala will run the show, temporarily blocking her ability to think rationally. It's unlikely she'll be able to hear the reassuring, rational words: "Don't worry, honey. That dog won't hurt you." She won't absorb this information because her amygdala is busy directing her focus to self-survival.

This survival instinct explains why it's almost impossible to reason with someone who's stressed or in distress. When in this condition, we can't think, but can only react. Once the crisis is over, our ability to think rationally returns.

For most of us, being emotionally hijacked brings about shocked, confused, or even bewildered responses. We end up saying things like:

- I'm really sorry. *(This is generally said while wondering what the heck we did wrong.)*

- Yes, Officer—or Yes, Your Honor.
- I don't know what came over me.
- I must have been out of my mind.
- It was an automatic response; I couldn't control myself.
- I don't understand—I always have my wits about me.

Joseph LeDoux, a neuroscientist in the Department of Psychology at New York University, posits that we have two brains, two minds, and two different kinds of intelligence: rational and emotional. Said another way, we have two minds: one that thinks and one that feels. And the one that feels works faster than the one that thinks.

Consider the situation with my aunt. When I heard the phone ringing for the fourth time within thirty minutes—before I could reason that the caller might not be an intruder bent on interrupting my evening—my amygdala sent an alarm to which I responded. I was ready to attack the next caller, just as surely as I would've reacted if someone broke into my home. As for my personal power, I lost it!

The fight-or-flight mechanism is a crucial biological trait that allows us to respond to danger, fear, and even anger. As mentioned above, this mind-body mechanism causes us to *feel* before we can rationalize a plan of action. It was most useful in the early days of human development, when our cave brothers and sisters frequently had to escape from dangerous predators. If someone spotted a snake or a tiger, then the fight-or-flight mechanism triggered a defensive response: we escape or act aggressively against the threat. This protective system literally saves our lives in emergencies and times of great danger. But the amygdala is *over*-equipped to handle traffic jams, lazy coworkers, nasty neighbors, and the like. These annoyances are definitely not fight-or-flight situations; however, in modern life we often move through our days on overdrive, overtaxing our natural defense system.

The amygdala is involved even in mundane situations. From time to time, we must apologize to a coworker, family member, or stranger for something we said or did. Maybe you were insensitive or flip. Maybe, in a fit of exasperation, you said you didn't have time to worry about their petty problems—you have problems of your own. Don't they understand? Later, you were embarrassed by what you said or did. Maybe you slammed a door on the way out. In that moment, your actions were automatic, as if you had no control over your rising rage. But now, after the dust has settled, you're painfully aware of how rude you were.

We all become obnoxious in situations that hijack our amygdala. Most of us have likely repeated the cycle many times throughout our lives. I remember my mother always telling me, "Kay, count to ten before you say or do anything! Take time to think." Do you suppose she knew about amygdala hijackings before the scientists?

ARE WE REALLY HELPLESS?

Knowing that brain mechanisms lead us to feel—and sometimes act—before we think is powerful information, but it doesn't help if we don't know how to correct or control unacceptable behavior. Mind you, this is about us. This isn't about controlling anyone else; it's about helping us to avoid embarrassing ourselves. Being able to control our behavior also helps us reclaim our power. Or as I prefer to say: take it back!

In his work on emotional intelligence, Goleman noted that individuals with high levels of self-awareness suffer less frequently from amygdala hijacking—more evidence that we need to be aware of personal power. Impolite or hostile behavior is a sure sign that personal power is draining away. "Amygdala storms," when our animal emotions take over, obliterate our sense of autonomy and choice.

Although our emotional reactions are automatic in these situations, Goleman believes we have tools to stop the downward cycle. It starts with awareness. Individuals in tune with themselves are more aware of the triggers that set them off. Therefore, increasing our awareness of "self" prevents us from experiencing an amygdala hijacking. So, how do we do that?

SELF-CARE LEADS TO SELF-AWARENESS

We want to increase our self-awareness, but the question is how. When I first learned about the process of amygdala hijacking, I initially had no idea where to begin. But then I remembered a certain acronym: H.A.L.T. The letters stand for: **H**ungry, **A**ngry, **L**onely, and **T**ired.

To prevent stress and rash behavior, the best self-care can be summed up as:

- Never get too **H**ungry.
- Never get too **A**ngry.
- Never get too **L**onely.
- Never get too **T**ired.

This acronym is used by many 12-step programs in which impulse control is important—for example, avoiding that first drink or hit or bite of food. Impulse control means not pulling into the casino or shopping mall when the checking account balance doesn't allow it. H.A.L.T. helps us stay away from destructive behavior of all kinds.

Let's be clear that amygdala hijacking occurs in degrees. Being rude or blowing up at a coworker, although embarrassing, isn't on the same level as the emotional storms that lead people to commit violence or physical abuse. While poor impulse control is related to criminal behavior, we're talking more about everyday situations.

It's important to review previous examples and examine what happened at the time of the amygdala hijacking. I remember the difficult day I'd had before the blow-up with my aunt. I often come home tired after a long day, but rarely will that alone lead to an amygdala takeover. Looking back at times when I acted inappropriately, I discovered that usually I was either very hungry or very tired—or both.

Hunger affects our blood sugar. For example, if our blood sugar is low, the body prioritizes to protect vital functions, such as blood pressure and the respiratory system. Over time, even after only a couple of hours, less energy is available to the brain. When people are hungry, they get cranky, to say the least. And as our blood sugar drops, we become vulnerable to making outbursts we later might not understand.

Being tired is also related to brain function. The cerebral cortex, which "rules" rationality and logic, is most active during the day. As the day turns to evening, the tired cerebral cortex loses influence and the limbic brain gains control. That's why a person on a diet can do great during the day but succumb to overeating in the evening. It's also no accident that most arguments and fights occur after dark, when we're literally not as rational. Most road rage occurs in the late afternoon rush hour, not the morning drive. When it comes to managing our personal power, we tend to do worse the more tired we get.

A self-aware person can predict when he'll be vulnerable and intervene accordingly:

- "Let's talk about our vacation plans over breakfast in the morning. I'm too tired. Plus, we both

- know we disagree about a lot of things, so our conversation won't go well now."
- "I'm not actually hungry. This intense craving feels real, but it's only just my fatigue talking. I'll take a hot bath and go to bed."
- "I want to talk about your school financing, but let's wait. I've had a long, hard day and am already on edge."

If we're self-aware, we can avoid problems and plan rather than react. Disagreements about vacation spots and college payments are common, even expected, issues in family life. But when we're tired, ordinary issues become heightened and sharpened in our mind, which cuts away at our ability to be rational.

LONELINESS—THE NEW NORMAL?

Fifty or so years ago, about one in ten households were made up of only one person. Today, about four in ten households are one-person homes. Divorce, delayed marriage, and death of a spouse are reasons cited for this change in the way so many live now. We must be careful, however, not to equate living alone with loneliness. Many people live alone by choice. In the past, more elderly parents moved in with their children—but we can't assume that everyone was happy about that arrangement. We can be lonely and disconnected even in the midst of family. Likewise, being alone isn't the same as being lonely. If we're self-aware, we can examine our feelings and try to find a satisfactory balance between being with others and being alone.

The American Association of Retired People commissioned a survey of individuals over age forty-five to assess loneliness among older adults. As predicted, married people report less loneliness than those who had never married. Perhaps more surprising was that 43% of younger people (25–49 years old) reported feeling lonely, but only 25% of those over age seventy said loneliness was an issue. Loneliness can affect us at any age.

Self-aware individuals tend to find the balance between sociability and solitude. When we're out of balance, we become vulnerable to amygdala hijacking—and losing our personal power in the process. Support groups and "affinity" groups can help soothe certain kinds of loneliness. For example, groups can provide an outlet for grieving individuals to talk about their feelings with others who understand. Sometimes family members and close friends aren't the best audience to hear about a person's loss. A grief group welcomes expressions of sorrow and loss, making participants feel less lonely with their feelings.

Those who feel strongly about an issue can find company among the likeminded. If you care about the environment, but your family is sick of hearing you talk about it, join the Sierra Club! Diet clubs help participants with weight-loss problems. And 12-step programs help millions cope with issues that once isolated them.

ANGER HIJACKING

Both underlying anger and angry episodes are forms of amygdala hijacking. Some people walk around mad—nothing ever goes right, everyone causes them trouble, and the world is an awful place. They tend to be on edge, and the rest of us avoid them and try not to set them off. However, walking on eggshells doesn't work in the long run; eventually they'll have an outburst. Perpetually angry individuals should seek counseling to help them resolve the issues that led to long-term anger.

THE BIG TWO

Of the four elements of the H.A.L.T. acronym, we're most vulnerable to amygdala hijacking when we're hungry and exhausted. The risk is amplified when we're hungry and tired at the same time—the late afternoon hours for many of us. How many of us have said, "I started the day off in a good mood—and then *he* called?" We might get upset about things that would've barely ruffled our feathers only hours before. But we can avoid emotional hijacking by understanding the way that hunger and fatigue affect us. This awareness makes a large contribution to our ability to manage our personal power.

HALT before you get hijacked.
– Kay Potetz, Ph.D.

9

ACTIONS AND REACTIONS

> A life of reaction is a life of slavery, intellectually and spiritually. One must fight for a life of action, not reaction.
>
> — RITA MAE BROWN

We're only human, we say, and our natural inclination is to trust people. Say you're about to make a large purchase. The rational side of you might want to wait a day or two before making a decision. But a taunting voice says, "This price is for a limited time only; buy now or you'll lose your opportunity for this great deal." Now you're hooked in. Even when our rational side hollers at us to *run, don't walk* away from a product or bargain (or medical and legal advice that doesn't sound quite right), we have difficulty heeding its advice. Why? We don't want to be left out, and we're uncomfortable saying no.

Social invitations can pose awkward dilemmas—and sometimes feelings get hurt. For example, say you receive an invitation to an event and your first inclination is to attend. But then a competing thought pops up: *Sally will be angry if I go.* To keep the peace, you decide to pass on the event and stay home. Or perhaps you don't want to travel to the graduation bash for your husband's third-cousin-twice-removed—but the pressure is on. Haunted by the specter of hurt feelings and family rifts, you spend your Sunday on a seventy-mile trip to the party and back. You're resentful, but you don't want to upset your spouse or hurt anyone's feelings.

MIRACLES, ELIXIRS, AND MAGIC POTIONS

I know few people who haven't been taken in by at least a couple of "miracle" products. Let's face it: most women find advertisements for anti-wrinkle cream seductive enough to stop channel surfing and listen to the miracle worker describe his product. It's guaranteed to take years off your appearance! Our dermatologist told us no such product exists, but then again, there's a different dermatologist on television showing us the before-and-after pictures. The internal argument begins:

The Voice: *You've tried this before once—no, twice. You were disappointed both times.*

You: *I know, I know. But this product sounds different. After all,* scientists *developed this product—it took* years *to come with the formula.*

The Voice: *Yeah, yeah. Keep your money in your pocket; you have better uses for it. Besides, you already have face creams—one for day, one for night, plus the one with the three-step process you never got the hang of.*

You: *They weren't like this one. It's an all-in-one product. No special serums. It's so convenient!*

The Voice: *What a chump you are.*

You: *Don't be such a killjoy.*

You might feel stubborn (in an argument with yourself, mind you) and immediately dial the 800 number—you'll get a bonus package if you call in the next fifteen minutes. Or you listen to the pitchman drone on . . . and soon your enthusiasm wanes. You sigh and keep channel surfing.

If you made the call and ordered the skin-care elixir, you aren't alone. Few of us can resist certain kinds of products from time to time, even when both our rational mind and our intuition tell us that they're too good to be true.

If you flipped to another channel, you probably were proud that you resisted being seduced away to a land of magic potions and the fountain of youth. You hung on to your power—and your money.

This is an everyday situation, one in which the consequences of giving in are small. Even if you bought the product and were disappointed, you paid a relatively small price for your gullibility. And to be fair, not all products sold in infomercials are fraudulent (although products that promise great skin or a great life are probably exaggerating). However, there are times when the consequences of giving in are much greater.

Here's the point: many of us give away our power because we want to appease authority. We're hesitant to challenge professionals—such as doctors or lawyers—or any other authority figure. When we feel infringed upon by someone in a powerful position, we sometimes fail to maintain our personal boundaries. And although we don't like making such mistakes, they give us a chance to see why emotional intelligence matters in these situations—and how we give away or hang onto to our power. A person will have many lapses in judgment over the course of their lifetime—some more serious and consequential than others.

THE AVOIDABLE MIX-UPS

When Paula left the hospital following major surgery, she was given prescriptions to fill during her convalescence. She read the labels after she arrived home and was ready to take her first round of meds, but she didn't recognize one of the drugs. This puzzled her, but she concluded that she must have misunderstood the home-care instructions. Still, she didn't remember the doctor or nurse mentioning this particular drug.

Hmm . . . maybe I should call the pharmacist, she thought. Nah, she'd done business at that drugstore before, and they were always so nice—and conscientious. Paula pushed her thoughts aside and swallowed the capsule. Later that night, she experienced dizziness so severe that she couldn't stand up. She called 911, and the EMTs took her to the emergency room. Initially, the doctors chastised her for "doing too much" after just being released from the hospital. Fortunately, though, a nurse in the ER recognized her symptoms as consistent with a harmful drug interaction.

Paula stayed in the hospital overnight, and the effects of the interaction eventually subsided. There was no serious or lasting harm. Later, the mistake was traced back to a mix-up of prescriptions originating in the hospital; it went unquestioned by the pharmacy because of an unusual staffing overlap. Many factors converged to cause this disaster.

Paula blamed herself for not asking about the unfamiliar drug and for questioning her memory. She later thought about the internal warnings that prodded her to call the pharmacy or the doctor. She had written off her uneasy feeling as "*irrational.*"

By not confirming that she was taking the right drug, Paula turned her power over to a nebulous "authority" outside herself. The doctor was trustworthy, the hospital stay had been uneventful, and she was familiar with the pharmacy. Therefore, her feelings must have been frivolous, so she brushed them away. She gave away her power because she wanted to trust these authority figures—and ended up in the hospital because of it.

Paula talked to friends and acquaintances about what happened and how she recognized the way she'd abdicated her power. She told her friends to pay attention to their feelings and to listen to the voices of intuition that protect us.

Paula's "mix-up" type of situation is very common. This kind of confusion results when we turn our power over to someone (or something) that we think has legitimate expertise or authority. Sometimes we fear the consequences of upsetting or insulting the authorities. But most of the time, we simply don't ask the questions that occur to us. Keep in mind that some mistakes and mix-ups are truly unexpected. We aren't losing power in situations over which we have no knowledge or control.

JUSTIN AND KRISTIN SEE THE DOCTOR

Justin, who'd gained about thirty-five pounds after he stopped smoking, finally agreed to go to the walk-in clinic for his fatigue and periodic chest pains. After taking a history, in which Justin described his stress at work, the doctor diagnosed the pain as psychological in origin—a result of overwork and a nervous reaction to the absence of the cigarettes he once used to manage his stress. The doctor recommended improving his diet to take off the extra pounds. Maybe relaxation and chewing gum would calm Justin's nerves. If the problem continued, though, the doctor said he'd run some tests, including routine blood panels.

After the short examination, Justin's wife, Kristin, joined her husband to listen to the doctor's recommendations. She was alarmed that the doctor hadn't taken any tests. She pointed out Justin's numerous cardiac risk factors. Her heartbeat picked up and her palms felt clammy. It had taken weeks to get Justin to even see a doctor, and now her concerns were being ignored. Shouldn't the doctor at least check Justin's cholesterol?

The doctor dismissed Kristin's concerns and implied that she was a worrywart—a typical wife fretting over her out-of-shape middle-aged husband. Embarrassed by the doctor's attitude toward her, she feared upsetting him—and Justin—by interfering. She kept quiet after they went home, but her anxiety didn't go away. It seemed like Justin became even more tired over the next few days.

Two weeks later, Justin collapsed at work. He was rushed to the hospital with heart attack symptoms and needed an emergency procedure to open a blocked artery. Fortunately, he recovered. Still, Kristin blamed herself for backing off, especially because the only reason she kept quiet was her fear of an authority figure: the doctor.

Who do we blame in this scenario? Justin could've spoken up for himself if he'd felt uneasy with the doctor's advice. Some would defend the doctor's evaluation of Justin's case history. These days, aren't we all concerned about *over*-testing?

Some might point the finger of blame at Kristin. Couldn't she have gotten Justin to seek a second opinion? But Justin might have ignored her or told her to stop nagging him. Ultimately, Justin was in charge of his health, not Kristin.

No one is truly at fault in this scenario. But Kristin will always wonder why she backed off so quickly—why she gave away her power the instant the doctor challenged her. Deeply afraid for Justin's health, she experienced true anxiety in the doctor's office that day. Her concerns and her feelings, were legitimate.

Those are only two examples, but we encounter situations like these all the time. You can probably think of a few on your own. Can you identify with any of the following?

- You agree to unfavorable terms in a contract because the attorney tells you, "It's the best we can do." Sure, she knows more than you do about the field, but you sense you're being hustled out of her office. Oh well, she's very busy and you don't want to take any more of her time. You leave her office with questions lingering in your mind.
- You sign a contract that you don't totally understand because you don't want the salesperson to think that you're dumb.
- Your neighbor invites you to a party. You agree to attend, even knowing that all her parties revolve around her latest product. She always pressures you to buy the product—and sell it to your friends, too. Last year it was cookware and vitamins; this year it's jewelry. You'd think she'd get the hint since you never sell any of her stuff. However, you don't want to offend a neighbor; after all, you live next door to her. But, somehow, going to the party makes you feel defeated. You could stop avoiding her if you told her outright that you aren't interested in her jewelry. But because you don't want to hurt her feelings, you keep your mouth shut and continue dodging her sales pitches.

- While a friend is giving you a ride home, she asks, "You don't mind if we stop at my son's house, do you? He lives on the way, and we'll only be there a few minutes." You know from experience that *a few minutes* means an hour or more of useless talk and listening to her grandchildren fight. You're really tired, and all you want is to get home and put on your pajamas. The honest answer to the question is, "No thanks, I'd rather go straight home." But you feel obligated because she's nice enough to give you a ride. You grudgingly agree to the visit, but you're upset with your friend for offering and with yourself for not having the courage to refuse.

What's going on in these situations?

In the first case, you gave away your power to someone who has greater expertise in a particular field. Like doctors, lawyers have authority, and many of us hesitate to challenge them—even when our internal voice tells us that something is off.

Going along when something doesn't feel right is a familiar experience; as children we were surrounded by authority figures—parents, teachers, coaches, minister, priests, rabbis, and so on—whom we had to obey. Sometimes we thought they were wrong or unfair, but we'd pay a heavy price if we confronted them. As young adults, we had to answer to professors, bosses, or commanding officers. Just the thought of confronting any of these authority figures usually made us nervous and apprehensive.

At the same time, we can't underestimate the strength of authority and expertise to do positive and beneficial things.

For example, we count on scientists, religious leaders, and teachers to build and improve societies all over the world.

In recent years, however, the nation was shocked by revelations about the sexual abuse of children by priests. When asked why they never told anyone, the victims, who are now adults, said that as children they were taught to obey and fear authority figures—and a priest is nothing if not an authority figure. This applies to teachers and coaches, too. Children fear being punished or called liars if they do confront an adult over any kind of wrongdoing.

As adults, we get into trouble when we hang onto these childhood fears. These feelings are often unreasonable, and we might not even be aware of their origin. Yet, we lose power every time we just go with the flow or ignore a quiet sense that something is wrong. I've known people who went along with poor suggestions that therapists gave them simply because they didn't want to risk making the therapist angry. Instead of discussing and sharing their concerns, they spent time and money on methods they didn't trust.

To be clear, I'm not arguing against listening to—and taking—expert advice. This is what we pay for, and professionals know far more than us about their specialty. However, no matter how much we want to trust them, we still need to check their advice against our gut feelings and speak up when we need to. We owe it to ourselves to remember that we're no longer children beholden to authority figures.

Almost everyone has encountered a character like the peddler-neighbor or the ride-giving friend. Both show us what happens when we give away our power because we don't want to hurt another person's feelings or make them dislike us. We agree grudgingly, as opposed to wholeheartedly, leading us to carry residual negative feelings. I believe this kind of ambivalent behavior begins around age two, when we first were told to be nice and get along with everybody. The behavior is then reinforced throughout childhood.

Few of us are taught how to ask for the things we want in life—or how to set and maintain personal boundaries. The dictionary tells us that a boundary is a line, point, or plane that indicates or fixes a limit or extent. Personal boundaries are the limits we set in relationships in order to protect ourselves. These boundaries are how we let others know what's acceptable and unacceptable to us. The relationship between our self-worth and our personal boundaries is directly proportional. In other words, the more self-worth we have, the more we're willing to establish and maintain personal boundaries that help us take care of ourselves.

I'm not suggesting that self-worth exposes the uncooperative monster within us, but rather that self-worth lets us tell people what's important to us—and what we're willing or not willing to do. Folks with low self-worth find themselves "going along just to get along," and they frequently end up doing things they'd rather not.

If you've ever said, "I *had* to go, I couldn't tell them no," or "What could I say?" you might want to examine your level of self-worth. Some of us routinely do things against our best interest in order to please others. My mom was always worried about what the "neighbors might think." With more mature eyes, I look back and realize that most of the neighbors were unlikely to care much about I did or didn't do. I know now that they had more pressing and important things on their minds than the Potetz family.

In her book, *Searching for You: Ideas about Healthy Relationships*, Suzanne Welstead explains that personal boundaries make it possible for us to separate our own thoughts and feelings from those of others and take responsibility for what we think, feel, and do. Boundaries allow us to enjoy our uniqueness while getting what we want and need in our lives.

Intact boundaries are flexible: they allow us to get close to others when it's appropriate. They help us maintain our distance when getting too close to someone who might hurt us. Personal boundaries allow us to distinguish the limitations of what we're willing to do.

For example, having clear personal boundaries lets us tell the neighbor that we really aren't interested in buying or selling her jewelry, but would enjoy having coffee sometime. The scenario with the ride-giving friend shows the importance of expressing our needs and sharing our personal boundaries on the spot. We need to get home and relax; we don't want to visit your son's house—maybe another time. The goal is to increase the external expression our self-worth, establish our boundaries, and share them with others.

It comes down to this: Is our neighbor's opinion so important that we'd sacrifice hours of our time doing something we don't enjoy? Does going along with a friend make us feel good about her? Probably not. Even if you like your neighbor and love your friend, your relationships will suffer in the long run if you worry about their feelings more than your own.

There's an easier solution that doesn't involve hiding from your neighbor or wasting an afternoon just to keep the peace. Simply tell people what you want—and stop wishing or hoping that they'll give you what you need. Stop assuming that people "just know" as if they can read minds.

> Boundaries: the importance of choosing to value ourselves. – Anonymous

Then we pivot to the next question: what will they think of me? We give away a tremendous amount of power by stewing about other people's perceptions. We were conditioned in childhood to always be nice; otherwise, catastrophic things would happen. Better to suffer in silence and go along. Consciously or unconsciously, we live by the motto: *Peace at any price.*

We also give personal power away when we act in a reactive way. Reacting includes these kinds of scenarios:

- agreeing to something just so others will think we're nice,
- allowing ourselves to be hustled out of a professional's office,
- signing a contract we don't quite understand,
- agreeing to sell your neighbor's jewelry,
- giving in to a friend.

There's something about the word "nice." We do so much to be thought of as nice, and we desperately hope that others will say nice things about us. We can't be called nice if we go around ruffling feathers, so most people comply and act passively with authority figures, friends, or even strangers.

Heaven forbid being proactive in the following ways:

- We tell the professional, "Before I leave, I have one more question."
- We're honest with the neighbor and firmly say we're not interested in selling jewelry.
- We tell our friend we need to go home and relax rather than spending the afternoon visiting.

In his book, *The 7 Habits of Highly Effective People,* Stephen Covey argues that we must be proactive instead of reactive, and he offers examples. Proactive people:

- take responsibility for their lives, realizing and accepting that everything else is out of their control;
- choose how they respond to stimuli: they're quite self-aware and understand how they're separate from their moods, feelings, and thoughts;
- have enough imagination to see beyond an unpleasant situation and make decisions based on their self-awareness;
- know how much they really control and are responsible for their thoughts and actions.

Examine the word "responsibility." It can be defined as having the ability to choose your own *response*. You could say that you're *response able*. Therefore, you can choose to be either proactive or reactive.

IDENTIFYING PROACTIVE AND REACTIVE ACTIONS

Put simply, being reactive is the opposite of proactive. *Reactive people give up control of their choices and let other people's behavior guide both their feelings and actions.* In our examples, reactive people end up selling their neighbor's jewelry (or spend a lifetime hiding from the neighbor), while *proactive people let their values drive their decisions.* They use their own values to decide how they'll respond.

When you understand the distinction between proactive and reactive, it becomes clear that no one can make you late, disappointed, or miserable without your consent. This might be a tough concept to accept, especially if you're accustomed to blaming your problems on bad luck or other people.

Covey says that once you can admit that "I am what I am today because of the choices I made yesterday," you can then declare, "I choose to be something else tomorrow."

THE LANGUAGE OF PROACTIVE AND REACTIVE BEHAVIOR

You can identify your tendency toward reactive and proactive responses when you listen to the words you choose. For example, if you say, "My officemate really gets to me," you're in reactive mode. You're letting someone else take control of your feelings and actions.

On the other hand, if you say, "I'm letting my officemate get to me, but I know I can choose my own response," you've shifted to proactive mode because you're taking responsibility for your feelings.

Once you're proactive, you can examine the situation, look at your perceptions and feelings, and find ways to handle the things that annoy you. For example, you could try to ignore the situation, ask the boss for a new officemate, or discuss your feelings with the problematic person. Proactive people keep all options on the table. If you really want to, you can quit your job and leave the situation altogether.

You have the power to exercise *any* of the above actions once you decide how to reach the best possible result. Exercising your power to be proactive is far more productive than reacting and saying things you wish you hadn't. Once you react with rancor, sarcasm, or blame, you can't take back your words.

If you find yourself saying things like, *I have to . . .* , or, *my hands are tied*, realize that you're using reactive responses and giving away your personal power. *I choose to . . .* is a proactive phrase indicating that you take full responsibility for your actions. This language reflects your understanding that you choose to make conscious decisions based on your values, not on fleeting or negative emotions.

If you want to develop a proactive stance in your life, try these four tips:

1. Pay attention to the words you and those around you use. How often do you hear the reactive expressions, "I have to . . . " or "I have no choice but to . . . ?"
2. Ask yourself, "What part of this situation can I control?"
3. Ask yourself, "What is my part in creating this situation?"
4. Watch the behavior of others. Then look inside yourself and decide how you want to respond to a similar situation. We can all learn from both positive and negative examples.

Try this for thirty days and see what happens. Let your watchword be *response able*, knowing that acting, rather than reacting, is critical in your quest to create a peaceful, fulfilling life.

10

SELF-RESPECT

> *When you are content to be simply yourself and don't compare or compete, everybody will respect you.*
>
> — Lao-Tzu

All our lives, we're told to respect others. My mother taught me to always respect my grandparents, my aunts and uncles, the neighbors, and every other adult that crossed my path. When I rode the bus as a small child, I always had to give my seat to an older person. My mother said it was to show respect. If my teacher did something I thought was unfair, I still had to show him respect because the teacher always was the boss.

I can almost hear you saying, "Yep, me too!" Rarely, if ever, did an adult ask for our side of the story. The few times we defended ourselves, we were told, "It's a hard lesson, but the world isn't always fair. In the long run, it's better to show respect and get along."

Even worse, if we spoke up about something an adult did, our words would be negated with admonishments like: "How can you say that about _____ (fill in the blank)? He/she would never do such a thing." Or we may have been told to quit telling stories. I believe being negated—having the truth as we see it simply wiped away—is one of the worst feelings a child can experience.

When I was young, teachers threatened that any act of disrespect would become part of my permanent record. That sounded ominous, as if something I did in third grade would keep me from being accepted by a college ten years later. I've been out of school for decades and have yet to see my so-called permanent record.

Adults spent a lot of time telling us how to act properly for others while listing the perils of disrespect. Little if any time was spent teaching us how to respect ourselves as we headed into our teens and beyond. Teenagers often act out in ways that reflect a lack of self-respect. They might dress provocatively, for example, or try alcohol and drugs, or use crude language (wherever did they learn it?)—knowing that adults will disapprove. After catching a teenager in the act, an adult might ask, "How could you do that? Where's your self-respect?" The answer to the question is often a blank stare.

As a child, I wasn't sure what self-respect was—I still don't know exactly how to define it. But I know that I would've answered that question with a blank expression, too. When parents teach their kids to respect others, they must explain that respect also means self-respect. Those who go through life with a healthy dose of self-respect will be much better at managing their personal power. They won't give it away, and they won't try to undermine others either. I've also noticed that individuals with self-respect tend to gravitate to each other, as if recognizing kindred spirits with whom they can feel safe and at ease.

Looking back into my childhood, I don't remember anyone teaching me about self-respect. The focus always was on how kids should respect the adults. We learned that there were rewards for staying out of trouble: adults would think we were nice and say pleasant things about us. The flipside of that—the humiliation of punishment and a rotten reputation—was very bad indeed.

We can conclude that most of us are intimately familiar with the concept of respecting others, but unaware of the need to respect ourselves. What a gap! For years I didn't realize the importance of self-respect and its direct relationship to personal power. Lacking self-respect, I was stuck feeling powerless and inferior to others. Further, if I didn't respect myself, how could I expect others to respect me?

TO BUILD SELF-RESPECT, START BY WATCHING YOUR MOUTH

There are many definitions of respect, and we could come up with examples from now until the end of time. So let's cut to the chase. Respectful behavior, however you define it, should be applied to yourself as well as others. For example, we might have dieted over the years with some successes and a few failures. How did you talk to yourself when you didn't lose as much weight as you wanted?

Your self-talk might have gone something like: "I can't lose weight. I've always been fat and always will be. I'm such a failure." Now let's say your best friend tried to diet, and that she, too, was unsuccessful. I bet you would tell her something more like this: "I know you've worked really hard on your diet, and I'm sure you're disappointed that you didn't lose more weight. But you're beautiful as you are, and I love you no matter what you weigh. You're a good person, and if losing weight is important to you, keep trying. I'll be here right beside you."

Compare the two responses and you'll find that we are much kinder to others than we are to ourselves. This is because of how we've been socialized. You know what I mean. How many times have you said to yourself, "All I need is more willpower. I need to stop being so lazy." You wouldn't think of saying that to a friend! Consider the damage done when you say nasty things to yourself.

Remember the "nitwit" we talked about in Chapter 3? Two file cabinets are inside your head: one holds all the cards listing the successes you've had in your life, and the other holds the cards listing your failures. The nitwit complies with anything you ask because he has no particular feelings about the orders you give him day in and day out.

When you say, "I can't do that," the nitwit shuffles through the negative files and finds a memory to support that fact. His response: "That's right, boss. You've screwed this up over and over, and you'll probably do it again." On the other hand, if you say, "Yes, I believe I can do that," he goes through the positive files and finds supporting data for that thought. This time, the nitwit has a much different response: "Yes boss. You've successfully done this many, many times—and you'll do it again."

Throughout our life, the nitwit reinforces the language we use with ourselves. This is why it's so important to pay attention to what you say to yourself—your self-talk. The nitwit agrees with anything you want him to, and your life moves toward that upon which you focus. Be as kind to yourself as you would your best friend. In other words, watch your mouth!

If you want to be respected by others the great thing is to respect yourself. Only by that, only by self-respect will you compel others to respect you.
— Fyodor Dostoyevsky

AVOID STEALING FROM YOURSELF

Every time you buy something you don't need—possibly adding to your already-exploding credit card debt—you're taking money (stealing) from your future self. Advertisers and marketers know what they're doing. They know the mental triggers that convince us we must have the latest kitchen gadget, dress, car, or tech gizmo guaranteed to make our lives hum along smoothly. Thousands lined up to buy the Apple iPhone 4S. Mind you, this occurred during an economic slump with the unemployment rate hovering just about 9%.

It's likely that some who bought the Apple iPhone 4S were unemployed. Oh well, what's a little more debt—especially when life will be great with your new iPhone. Everybody has one, and you'd feel so left out and jobless if you didn't have one, too. Besides, you can always declare bankruptcy or blame the system for your financial debacles. Instead, take your power back and make financial decisions that are in *your* best interest, not in the false image you're trying to maintain—with the nitwit's help.

This sounds terribly judgmental, but I truly believe that we never build self-respect if we strive to impress others with external displays of status or power, or if we foolishly emulate the lifestyles we see on TV. When we live thinking about what things look like from the outside, we know the price of everything and the value of nothing.

> *Before you try to keep up with the Joneses, be sure they aren't trying to keep up with you.*
> – Anonymous

RECOGNIZE WHEN PEOPLE DISRESPECT YOU AND TAKE STEPS TO STOP IT

People with self-respect don't allow others to treat them badly and prefer not to associate with disrespectful people. Without self-respect, we might willingly take someone's abuse because we believe that they don't know any better, leading us to adopt a superior, self-righteous attitude. Or, we might allow disrespect because we're afraid the other person will get angry and end the relationship, calling into question our sense of our own worth.

Many people believe they don't *deserve* to be treated well and are worried—even nervous and fearful—about making other people angry. In other words, they keep their mouths shut and go along with whatever is happening to them, no matter how disrespectful. This might seem like a great strategy to keep the peace, but only rarely does it get anyone what they want or need from others over the long haul. Staying silent about disrespectful behavior also doesn't do much for one's self-esteem.

To build self-esteem, we must define our personal boundaries and share them with others. It's okay to make statements such as:

- "That comment really hurt my feelings; please don't say that again."
- "When we agree to meet for dinner at 6:00 p.m. and you show up thirty minutes late, I feel taken for granted. My time is just as important as yours. The next time you're late for dinner, I'll wait for fifteen minutes. After that, I'm leaving the restaurant."
- "Never returning my phone calls is unacceptable. I won't stay in this relationship if I always have to do the calling."
- "Please stop saying negative things about my . . . (husband, son, daughter, mother, friend, and so forth). I know that sometimes they don't treat me fairly, but hearing mean comments about them hurts me and just makes me feel worse."
- "Please don't bring up the past. What's done is done. Let's move forward."
- Instead of "Don't you think it's a little chilly in here?" state your need in a straightforward way:

"Would you please close the window a little bit? I'm feeling chilly."

The above examples erase the possibility that others will misunderstand your needs. Furthermore, "I didn't know that's what you meant" statements become null and void and are exposed as attempts to reduce your personal power. The *take it back* response might be: "What did you think I meant when I said, 'Would you please close the window a little bit?' I'm feeling chilly." Delivered in a calm, quiet voice, this statement reinforces your stated boundaries and well-deserved self-respect. How can anyone become angry at such an innocent question?

Directly telling people what we need and how we feel is a powerful strategy. *Hoping* someone notices and fulfills your needs is self-defeating and annoying; further, it does nothing to build your self-respect. I believe others when they ask, "Why didn't you tell me you were cold or hot or tired, and so forth?" My needs are generally not the focus of other people, and some people are nonobservant and clueless.

I'm not suggesting that we should care only about ourselves and ignore the thoughts and feelings of others. Quite the opposite. Look at it this way: the more we're in touch with and express our personal needs, the greater our self-respect. This takes on momentum of its own and directly relates to building and maintaining personal power.

The language we use sets a tone for the way we communicate with ourselves and each other. Too often we use weak phrases such as:

- I can't.
- I should.
- If only . . .
- It's not my fault.

- It's a problem.
- What will I do?
- Life's a struggle.

Listen to yourself and see if you can replace weak phrases with ones that convey strength, such as:

- I won't.
- I will.
- Next time.
- My part in this is . . .
- It's an opportunity.
- I can handle it.
- Life's an adventure.

When you change your language, you change your internal attitude, and this is reflected in the way others respond to you.

NEVER A VICTIM OR A RESCUER BE

It seems like victims will always find a rescuer and rescuers will always find a victim. Many years ago I had a friend who was in the middle of a divorce. She had a problem teenager (alcohol and other drugs) and very little money. Oh, how I wanted to help and support Esther—and, sure enough, she always needed my backing. If Esther needed money, I'd give her a loan; if Esther was depressed, I'd listen to her sad story; if Ester wanted to talk about her son, she'd call and I'd offer warmth and support. After all, she was in the middle of a divorce. What I finally realized was that I was more worried about Esther and her problems than she herself was.

Why did I put up with this, you ask? I stayed hooked in because Esther always said persuasive things. "I don't know what I'd do without your friendship," she'd say, or "Thank heaven for people like you." Although I found her constant complaining tiresome, I liked hearing how helpful and important I was. I felt so needed.

Sometimes Esther would call and cry to me for almost an hour. What part did I play here? I stayed on the phone with her for far too long. But I couldn't tell her I couldn't talk to her. After all, she needed me!

After about six months of this, I noticed that Esther, who'd borrowed money from me, went out with friends more often than I did. She even took off to Las Vegas for a "much-needed" getaway weekend. Yep, my broke friend could afford a vacation. That's when I realized that I had blown the situation out of proportion. I was getting nothing out of the relationship, except for her telling me that I was great!

One afternoon, Esther kept me on the phone (notice how passive I was) for an hour. She wore me down until I felt depressed—but later I learned she went to the movies with another friend and didn't invite me to join them. Of course she felt better; she'd dumped all of her problems on me, while I accepted them as though they were my responsibility. What was wrong with this picture?

After this wakeup call moment, I concluded that, over a period of six months, Esther had done nothing to improve her lot in life. Everything that happened to her was horrible: oh you poor thing, that's so awful, and so forth. I went along with the scenario, putting my needs on hold and always worrying about her. But then I saw the insanity in my behavior. I wasn't actually helping Esther. Instead, I gave away my personal power—which, by the way, did nothing to help her. She didn't need to worry about her life; I was doing that for her. No sense in everybody being upset.

I had no ability to actually change her situation. She agreed to everything I suggested but never followed through. I had to face a simple fact: I had no control over what she did or didn't do. However, I did have power over my own behavior. I decided to *take back* my personal power. First, I established some boundaries by asking her to stop calling after 9:00 p.m. because I needed my rest. I spoke up when I was too busy to stay on the phone and stopped her from rehashing the same story over and over again. Furthermore, I stopped loaning her money, even though she'd become dependent on my infusions of cash.

I changed my behavior in other ways, too. When Esther talked about all her dilemmas, I asked what she intended to do about them. I no longer sympathized with her, nor did I agree with her negative view of the world. Through my experience with Esther, I learned that sympathy doesn't help anybody; it only keeps a weak person weak.

How did Esther respond to my newly found self-respect? As you can probably guess, she wasn't gracious. "How can you do this to me when I'm in such a mess?" she howled—and that was just the opening salvo. What would she do without me as a sounding board? Who could she talk to? Who would help her if I didn't? Esther was so convincing that she almost had me worried. But I came to my senses. Nothing would change until I changed. Guess what? Esther moved on. She found others in whom to confide and ultimately did just fine.

For a while, I saw myself as a victim. Look how Esther took advantage of me! She was unfair, self-absorbed, and a bad friend. Finally, I admitted to myself that Esther took advantage of me with *my* permission. We couldn't have had this unsatisfying six-month drama unless I played my role. When I quit playing along, Esther stopped taking advantage of me. That was a bitter cup of tea to swallow, but it was true, whether I liked it or not. I was responsible for my dysfunctional friendship with Esther.

THEN AND NOW

Esther's problems are now in the past, but I learned from the ordeal. The more I stay true to myself, the more I see that I've always been in charge of my relationships—be they draining and dismal or rich and fulfilling. My negative choices with Esther led me to self-destructive behavior and gave me a bad feeling in the pit of my stomach. This wasn't a fluke either; I've always been in charge of my thoughts, feelings, and actions. With Esther, I made bad choices—until I found my self-respect and changed my behavior.

Now, before I speak or commit to something, I clarify what I really think and feel. I make commitments only after truly feeling peaceful about them. I know I won't compromise my needs or values to gain the approval of others. I put self-care first and make time each day for self-reflection and inner connection. Regardless of other people and things that need my attention, I take care of myself first. I do this because when I'm physically and mentally healthy, I really have something of value to offer others. Yep! *I took it back, my power that is.*

THE DEEP REWARDS OF SELF-RESPECT

Self-respect means knowing that you deserve respect and dignity and success and happiness and love as much as every other living being on the planet. What prevents us from accepting such a basic premise? If we keep looking to others for permission to feel equal, happy, and deserving, then we'll never develop the self-respect that guides constructive, fulfilling behavior.

So, stop looking outside of yourself for affirmation and know on the inside that you're worthy of self-respect. Believe in yourself. As you do so, your self-esteem will rise and you'll be comfortable with yourself regardless of who's around.

Once you're comfortable with yourself, all sorts of people will respect you for who you are. You'll find yourself on solid terrain that will never betray you, no matter the circumstances.

Nobody can make you feel inferior without your permission.
– Eleanor Roosevelt

11

I'M SORRY, YOU'RE SORRY—OR ARE WE?

> There's one sad truth in life I've found
> While journeying east and west—
> The only folks we really wound
> Are those we love the best.
> We flatter those we scarcely know,
> We please the fleeting guest,
> And deal full many a thoughtless blow
> To those who love us best.
> — **Ella Wheeler Wilcox**

Let's start with a truism: some apologies are easy; some apologies are hard. If my grocery cart collides with yours, I have no problem telling you I'm sorry. Most of us don't lose face—or personal power—by giving a simple everyday apology to a stranger. More times than not, the stranger will apologize, too. There are a few exceptions, of course: some people have bad manners, while others can't admit even tiny mistakes. Overall, though, it's easy for us to express a heartfelt apology to someone we don't know well, especially if the incident itself is trivial.

On the other hand, many of us find it difficult to sincerely apologize to those closest to us. In fact, we are often more polite and pleasant to strangers than we are to our family and close friends. If we accidentally collide with a family member, for example, we may even tell him to watch where he's going. "It makes me nuts," we snarl, "when you don't pay attention and bump into me."

Now, our loved one may not exactly be sorry, and he might reply, "Well, excuse me for breathing. I didn't realize you owned the sidewalk."

We frequently resort to sarcasm and impoliteness with family members. We might defend this by saying that it's okay to let our guard down and be more casual around those we know. By this argument, familiarity really does breed contempt! This isn't a good setup for a pleasant family life or friendship, and it doesn't make for a harmonious workplace either.

In a 2010 article in the *Wall Street Journal*, journalist Elizabeth Bernstein reported on research conducted by a group of Canadian psychologists. According to their findings, adults apologize about four times per week. However, on average, they apologize more frequently to strangers (22% of the time) than to romantic partners (11%) or family members (7%).

Most children are taught the importance of apologies. I can still hear my mother saying, "Tell Mrs. Minnick that you're sorry." And whether I believed I did something wrong to our next door neighbor or not, I had to utter the words, "I'm sorry." How unfair!

To extract a little self-satisfaction out of my circumstances, I started apologizing with a sneer or slightly sarcastic tone in my voice. If this sounds familiar, it's because many of us had to apologize for things that, in our childhood minds, were most unjust. However, we don't necessarily change this way of thinking as we move out of childhood and adolescence. Rather than sorting out situations from an adult perspective, we get stuck in the past; we continue to hate giving apologies and usually feel that we're being treated unfairly. This is how the insincere apologies that adults use—aka wisecracks and sarcasm—are born and nurtured. Old habits are difficult to change, and being unaware of your own behavior compounds the problem.

Self-awareness is required for high emotional intelligence, and in turn, emotional intelligence strongly influences the way we use—or misuse—our personal power. Part of self-awareness is having the ability to feel genuine remorse about making a mistake or hurting another person. We must develop this capacity and exercise it as we would a muscle.

WHEN "I'M SORRY" IS A PREAMBLE

Never ruin an apology with an excuse.
– Kimberly Johnson

We often complicate our apologies because of how difficult it is to take responsibility for ourselves and admit when we're wrong. A sincere apology is a true exercise of personal power, but too many of us are embarrassed to admit regret or remorse. For some people, saying "I'm sorry" is only a preamble, a formality, the beginning of the sentence. Do you sometimes hear a certain inflection in person's voice and know that a "but" is on the way? For example, you've probably heard a "but" apology that goes something like: "I'm sorry if what I said made you feel bad. But I just couldn't believe that you did something so stupid."

The "but" tells you to forget everything that was said up to that point—now the real truth is coming. There are other forms of sarcastic apologies, such as: "I'm sorry, but I can't drop everything each time you call for something." Wouldn't it be more powerful to say, "I'd like to help, but I can't right now; how about at a time more convenient for both of us?"

Our personal power diminishes when we avoid sincerely apologizing for mistakes. Taking a defensive posture eats up our energy and keeps us chewing over ways to avoid the truth. For example: "This wouldn't have happened if you had . . . (You fill in the rest)," or "Why don't you ever listen to me? Now everything is messed up."

Unqualified apologies clear the air and bring an acceptable end to most everyday conflicts. For example, not long ago I agreed to give a friend an early morning wakeup call. She had an alarm clock but was afraid she'd oversleep and miss a very important appointment. Being an early riser myself, I didn't hesitate to agree to call her. Knowing I'd be up at that time, calling her posed no problem for me. The next morning came—and I promptly forgot to call. Oh dear! When I realized what I had done, I was afraid that she had overslept. What could I tell her? I couldn't tell her the truth: that I forgot to call her. Maybe I could tell her I was sick and overslept myself, or better yet: "There was a family emergency! I wasn't at home in the morning, so I couldn't call you."

What baloney! Not only did I fail to do a favor for a friend, now I was figuring out ways to lie about it. Talk about giving all of my power away—this was all that and more. I was going to position myself as powerless, which would've cast a shadow on my credibility.

Thankfully, I came to my senses in the nick of time and told my friend the plain truth. "I'm so sorry I forgot to call you this morning. I hope you didn't oversleep. I should've written myself a reminder note. I hope you'll understand and accept my apology."

> *An effective apology focuses more on compassion for the victim than redemption for the offender.*
> – John Kador

If a conflict still requires resolution, both parties should handle it non-defensively. Unfortunately, heartfelt apologies are not as common as we'd like to think. In her *Wall Street Journal* article, Bernstein described the different kinds of apologies defined by the Canadian researchers. They'll probably sound familiar to you.

THE DEFENSIVE APOLOGY: By definition, a defensive apology is insincere and disingenuous; it's a self-protective maneuver meant to defend one's actions or words. It's probably the most common type of apology. A conversation that leads to a defensive apology would go something like this:

Joe: *You always forget to enter the amount of the checks you write. It's driving me crazy.*

Mary: *C'mon. You know that's not true.*

Joe: *It is true. You're not exactly a financial wizard, you know . . .*

Insulted, Mary walks away hurt and angry. Any number of things could happen next. For example, a few hours later, Mary could confront Joe and tell him he owes her an apology. Or Joe could grow tired of the cold-shoulder treatment and go to Mary on his own. Either way, this is what would transpire:

Joe: *I'm sorry if what I said made you feel bad, but I couldn't believe you did something so stupid.*

Mary: *Great, now I'm stupid.* She throws up her hands and walks away.

For his part, Joe might mutter, *I apologized, didn't I? What more does she want?*

Mary and Joe could eventually argue this out "on the facts." Is Mary a financial dunce or not? Is she ungracious because she won't accept the non-apology apology? Is Joe a jerk, or does he lack tact in stating the obvious? No one wins arguments like this, and in terms of personal power, everyone loses. Most family disagreements eventually end (at least for the moment) because life goes on and the parties tire of the tension. But the issues at stake remain unresolved.

In the above example, Joe defended his accusation. He wasn't actually sorry about what he said; he just wanted peace in the house, so he offered a lame apology. Defensive apologies always make a bad situation worse.

THE STRATEGIC APOLOGY: This semi-sincere apology is used to end a fight or to soothe someone's anger, but only when we believe we haven't done anything wrong. It goes something like this:

Barry: *Here's the deal. We missed our deadline, and Steve over at PrintRight can't deliver the conference programs on Thursday. They'll overnight them and we'll have them Friday morning. It's the best they can do.*

Four pairs of eyes turn to Beverly. They all know she failed to deliver the proofed copy of the program on time. Beverly doesn't like the stares she's getting. None of this was her fault. She had problems with the kids at home; she had to buy groceries for her sick neighbor. How was she to know that

PrintRight had a 10:00 p.m. delivery deadline and missing it would add a full day to the project's timeline?

Beverly: *Hey, don't look at me. It's not my fault.*

Barry: *It's not about blame, Bev, but delivering the proofed program was your responsibility. Now we have to work around the delay.*

Beverly notices that people are staring into space to avoid looking at her. Embarrassed, she wants to get this problem behind her.

Finally, Beverly adds: *Okay, okay, I'm sorry. Let's move on.*

Silence follows Beverly's impatient tone. Barry knows that her apology is insincere, and he's well aware that Beverly doesn't want to take responsibility for her mistake—she seldom does. As her supervisor, Barry needs to address what is growing into a pattern: her constant mishaps and rushing to meet deadlines.

Beverly: *You're right, so can we just end this now?*

Everyone in the meeting eventually figures out how to solve the problem created by the delay. It looks as if they've moved on, but they've only delayed the issue. Beverly's coworkers will need to change their plans for registering conference attendees. They're annoyed at Beverly because of her weak apology. Down the road, these resentments will resurface. Beverly's strategic apology failed to defuse the core problem and left behind issues to be solved at a later time.

We lose personal power when we offer grudging, non-apology apologies designed to end an uncomfortable moment. We seldom admire those who deny responsibility for the repercussions of their mistakes. The atmosphere at the staff meeting would've been far different had Beverly offered a heartfelt apology for the problem she created and tried to be part of the solution. However, Beverly was so caught up in making excuses for herself—to herself—that she didn't have the mental energy to explain the reasons she failed to complete the task on time. Had she done so, she might have found allies around the table. Coworkers can be forgiving and cooperative when someone takes responsibility for their mistakes.

THE CONTINGENT APOLOGY: This kind of apology sometimes becomes infamous—we often hear it from those whose mistakes are "caught on tape," so to speak. It's a favorite among politicians, entertainers, and other public figures who have made disparaging comments about things like religion, ethnicity, gender, sexual orientation, personal characteristics, and even disabilities. First, they deny that their comments were at all negative; when that doesn't end the dustup, they apologize to those who "misinterpreted" their words and "happened" to be offended. They take care not to actually say they're sorry for making the stupid, offensive remarks in the first place. Here's a sample:

I sincerely apologize if my impromptu comments about _____ (fill in the blank) *offended anyone.*

If the off-color joke I told in good fun made anyone uncomfortable, then I'm sorry.

I mistakenly sent that email about _____ (fill in the blank) *to the "wrong" list. It was meant to be private, but if others were upset, then I apologize.*

The operative word is *if*. In these apologies, they fail to take back their words or actions. Sometimes they'll plead ignorance or try to minimize the effect or claim that the whole thing was a joke. Whenever an incident makes the evening news, the contingent apology usually keeps the issue in the headlines and becomes a topic of conversation or debate. Sometimes the apology exacerbates the original problem. When we hear that an insulting email was sent to the so-called "wrong" list, it leaves us wondering about the "right" list.

Of course, the contingent apology is not limited to the public sphere. Joe could easily "apologize" to Mary by saying:

I'm sorry if you were offended when I suggested that you always screw up our checking account and are stupid when it comes to money.

Can't you feel the love? I'm sure Mary feels much better now.

Or, Beverly could use the contingent apology with her coworkers:

I'm sorry if anyone is inconvenienced by the delivery delay.

She's denying her responsibility; somehow the "delivery delay" has become a completely unconnected event, totally out of her hands. Besides, there's no "if" about whether the team was inconvenienced. Addressing the fallout of Beverly's mistake is exactly why the staff meeting was convened in the first place. Ignoring that fact, Beverly is basically saying: *If I inadvertently was involved in something that caused us problems, I apologize.*

This "apology with qualifications" always reinforces a belief in our innocence and portrays us as the victim, as in:

My remarks were taken out of context, and people shouldn't think the worst. Why are so many people overly sensitive these days, anyway?

Meanwhile, Joe and Beverly can feel like the "good guys":

At least I apologized, they smugly conclude.

THE BULLY APOLOGY: This apology is entirely insincere and has no redeeming qualities. It's used as a "Band-Aid" fix when delivering a caustic message.

Bully Boss: *Sorry to dump this big fat report on your desk just as you're ready to go home. But I need your recommendations first thing in the morning.*

Employee: *What? You're just getting this to me now. It's going to take hours of reading and analysis.* The employee mentally sees himself cancelling dinner plans and losing sleep.

Bully Boss: *Don't blame me—I said I was sorry. What do you want from me?"*

This is obviously not an apology, but is really the opposite: it shuts down any potential response. In this example, the only sure way to counter the bully apology is to ignore it or head it off by opening a negotiation about the timeline. People use this apology simply because it works to defuse someone else's anger. It's manipulative and uses pseudo-power to make a point. For sure, this sarcastic, "so-sue-me" style of apology is not a sign of a self-aware individual.

THE TOO-LATE APOLOGY: Days, months, or even years after an ugly event, a person might come to us and express sincere regret, as in, *I realize now that what I did was wrong.* In a sense, this apology is too late; whatever harm was done can't be undone. This is especially true of crimes or other serious infractions with long-lasting or permanent consequences. If a small mistake is involved, then most people accept the apology because it was sincerely delivered. We also can make a "better late than never" argument here.

THE HEARTFELT APOLOGY: According to the Canadian psychologists, we can evaluate apologies on a scale of least to most sincere. We've analyzed of the different kinds of insincere apologies, but some apologies are heartfelt and show emotional intelligence:

I'm so sorry. I understand that I hurt you. It won't happen again.

This is an earnest and well-intentioned mea culpa. It communicates an understanding of the pain inflicted and regret for causing it. It also contains the promise of change. *It won't happen again* is a big statement, a mature realization that the mistake—whatever it was—isn't acceptable.

The heartfelt apology would've saved Joe and Mary a great deal of hurt. For example, Mary could've apologized for making the checkbook mistake—which did in fact cause a temporary problem—and Joe could've avoided attacking her character: "She always does this."

Imagine the change in atmosphere at the staff meeting if Beverly had thought through what happened and stopped making internal excuses that left her blameless. By being honest with her coworkers, she could've grown as an individual and as a professional team member:

I dropped the ball here, and I'm sorry that my mistake means that we have to change our conference plans. I'll help in any way I can to make this easier, and I won't let it happen again.

Contingent apologies are never heartfelt if the person doesn't fully admit their mistake. Not long ago, I unintentionally hurt a friend's feelings. I didn't realize it at first, and when I learned how my friend felt, I had to think about what I'd say. In short, I had to put myself in my friend's shoes and understand her point of view. The next day I called and apologized—no ifs, no qualifiers, and no defensive posturing. I simply said I was sorry. My friend accepted the apology, and that was that.

There are times when a person must admit to their insensitivities and rethink certain attitudes and beliefs. If you notice your apologies are laced with "ifs," then consider the seedy agenda that you're projecting. Why are you defending yourself? Are you genuinely sorry for your mistake? Internally, take down your defensive walls and stop wasting your personal power by making excuses for yourself.

THOUGHTS ON APOLOGIES

If you need help with your own apologies, Bernstein supplies us with the following list:

- Know and understand what you did wrong. If you're not sure, ask those involved. Find out how your actions look from another point of view.
- If others ask if they've offended you, tell them the truth. Don't assume that they know what they did to hurt or harm you. We don't always know what we've done wrong.
- Show real remorse. If you say, "I'm sorry you're hurt," you're implying the person is too sensitive. Take total responsibility and say, "I'm sorry I hurt you." Admit you caused the hurt.
- Avoid a defensive posture, especially "but," as in, "I'm sorry, but . . ." This often inflames a situation and brings the hurt back. For example, Joe doesn't score points with his accusatory, non-apologetic attitude, which essentially says, "I'm sorry about what I said, but I couldn't believe that you'd do something so stupid."
- Sincerely offer to make changes. Commit to avoid making the same offense again.
- Don't throw in the kitchen sink. If you're the one who wants an apology, stick to the matter at hand. Don't bring up past slights.
- Don't delay. Just do it. An imperfect, but heartfelt apology is better than no apology at all.

Think of people you admire most—not just like or love, but admire. Do they take responsibility and apologize when they know an apology is in order? Part of what you admire about them is their ability and emotional maturity. They likely have a high level of emotional intelligence, which brings about the kind of self-awareness that allows them to apologize for mistakes without losing personal power.

12

LEAVING BEHIND THE "THEY" MENTALITY

> *I wondered why somebody doesn't do something about that. Then I realized I'm somebody.*
> — Lily Tomlin

At one time or another, we've all fallen into the "they" mentality: blaming a vague, undefined group of people and holding them responsible for personal grief and society's ills. It's easy to gripe when we can point the finger of blame away from ourselves. You know what I mean:

- Why don't *they* put a stop sign in that dangerous intersection?
- Why don't *they* clean up corruption in city government?

- When is *somebody* going to do something about food prices?

But say some casual observer asks us if we've called our city council about the stop sign. Have we talked to our neighbors about the corruption that's poisoned our community? Have we given our support to efforts to solve these problems? In other words, who exactly is "they?" Can we name the people who should get to work and solve these problems?

I don't claim for a minute that we can get fast results by speaking up about something as complex as food prices. Some problems are too difficult for easy answers. However, men and women just like us worked hard and made real change, starting food banks, soup kitchens, community gardens, and food co-ops that benefit millions of people.

Jumping into the fray is one good way to use our personal power. We can't solve every problem alone, but we can help those already working on the issue at hand. No one has singlehandedly saved a prairie or cleaned up a river or won the right to vote. On the other hand, people with self-respect don't wait for others to step up to the proverbial plate. I don't know about you, but I can't imagine Susan B. Anthony saying, "*Someone* ought to give women the right to vote." Likewise, it's unlikely Jonas Sauk sat around all day wondering why *they* didn't develop a polio vaccine.

When we try to right a wrong or solve a problem, our actions have consequences. We choose what we want to do. If we join every group that comes along, though, our personal power will drain away. I'm not suggesting that we hoist all the burdens of the world on our shoulders. However, our perspective changes when we stop waiting for others and instead take action in the world. Maybe we organize a group to clean up the park down the street or join a watchdog group to raise community awareness. We're not tackling the impossible, after all. Responsible citizens do this kind of thing all the time because they get tired of waiting.

Candace Lightner, better known as Candy, spearheaded one of the most powerful movements in our country. Who is Candy Lightner, you ask? Most people don't recognize her name, but she's the woman who founded Mothers Against Drunk Driving (MADD). Lightner changed our society in incredibly important ways. If you happen to be under age thirty, or even forty, you may not know that just one woman started MADD. She's been called a hero, a crusader, even an angel.

When she started her work, it was for personal reasons. First, a drunk driver rear-ended Lightner's car, and her daughter, Serena, was slightly injured. However, six years later, her son, Travis, was run over by driver impaired by tranquilizers. Travis was left in a coma with broken bones and other injuries, including permanent brain damage. The driver never received so much as a traffic ticket.

As if that weren't enough, in 1980, Candy Lightner's thirteen-year-old daughter, Cari, was killed by a drunk driver. The driver hit Cari, passed out, then woke up and drove away. Two days before this crime, the driver (a repeat DWI offender) had been released on bail for a hit-and-run drunk driving accident, his fifth offense in four years.

Four days after she lost Cari, Candy Lightner started MADD. She'd learned the drunk driver would probably not go to prison for his crime. Later, Lightner would explain that she felt compelled to turn this senseless homicide into something meaningful. Slowly but surely, MADD raised public awareness about the problem of impaired drivers, who were usually intoxicated on alcohol or other drugs. As astonishing as it seems now, being drunk was often considered an excuse for an accident, as in: "I can't be held responsible because I was impaired." (As if the impairment was "just one of those things." It happened, but no one's to blame.) Therefore, these impaired drivers were often not held accountable.

Lightner changed all that by putting faces on the victims—our parents, children, siblings, friends, coworkers, and so on. Statistics of drunk-driving fatalities are dry and abstract, but the faces of the victims, some of them infants and toddlers, moved hearts and minds. Lightner and her organization succeeded in moving people—and prompting new legislation. Since 1980, state legislatures changed and strengthened laws dealing with impaired driving. These included raising the legal drinking age from eighteen to twenty-one in states that hadn't already done so. Over time, states also changed the standards for blood alcohol levels, lowering the legal limit. Because of MADD, we have the concept of designated drivers, and now the law requires jail time for those who injure or kill another person while impaired. Because of Lightner's work, government commissions were created and charged with educating the public about impaired driving. Today, in large part because of Lightner, everyone knows about the dangers of drinking and driving.

Today, MADD is bigger than Candy Lightner or any one individual, but it didn't exist before she started it. The first members to join were families who had lost loved ones to impaired drivers, but as the years have passed, the issue became mainstream and is now supported by the vast majority of U.S. citizens.

CANDACE LIGHTNER AND THE EMOTIONAL CARBON FOOTPRINT (EFC)

Candy Lightner did more than change laws. Her relentless work as the founder of MADD raised our intellectual awareness of an issue that also touched our hearts. Some of us remember when President Ronald Regan gave her the Presidents Volunteer Action Award, or watched the 1983 NBC made-for-television movie, *Mothers Against Drunk Drivers: The Candy Lightner Story*. Lightner has also expanded her horizons and used her reputation and influence in other positive ways. For example, being half Lebanese, she has served as President of the American-Arab Anti-Discrimination Committee.

The next generation of Lightners found new ways to spread the word about drunk driving. Candy's daughter, Serena, founded Students Against Drunk Driving (SADD), now known as Students Against Destructive Decisions. Like MADD, SADD has chapters throughout the country.

Candy Lightner is still alive, but she has already left her mark on history. I think of her as a person with a positive Emotional Carbon Footprint. I can hear you asking, "What the heck is that?" Let me explain. In 2009 I wrote an article, "What's Your Emotional Carbon Footprint (ECF)?" for the *PADONA Journal*, a publication for Pennsylvania nurses. In that article, I compared the scientific theory of our carbon footprint—the disastrous effect that "dirty" energy has on our environment—with what I've labeled our Emotional Carbon Footprint (ECF).

Candace Lightner left behind a legacy that goes beyond just the facts. Her quest, begun while suffering a profound loss, has earned our admiration. She's a modern-era example of someone who acted rather than wondering why others—they—didn't fix the problem.

Unless we're hermits, we exchange emotions with every person we encounter, every day we're alive. Emotions are contagious, and we leave behind our ECF wherever we go. Whenever I meet someone new, their impression of me is recorded in their amygdala. The feeling of this experience is retrieved whenever he or she is reminded of our encounter. This is critical, because we might forget names, occupations, or hometowns, but we always remember how other people left us feeling. This is our ECF: the quality of the feeling we leave behind.

AN ECF FOR THE AGES

If you're looking for someone with a long-lasting ECF, I can think of no one better than Abraham Lincoln. In April of 2011, there were many commemorations of the 150th anniversary of the start of the U.S. Civil War, a hideous conflict that divided our nation into two warring halves. In 1865, after four years of fighting, there were 620,000 soldiers dead and hundreds of thousands more coping with life-changing wounds. Our Civil War was bloodier than any other conflict in American history, and it left a terrible legacy we still struggle to overcome. After the anniversary, many articles, assessments and opinions were written about the war and its participants, from soldiers to generals to citizens on both sides. No matter how we assess the war from the long view of history, we know that Lincoln accepted responsibility and tried as hard as he could to keep the Union together.

One of the 2011 articles I read about Lincoln and the Civil War is called *The Surprising Global Reach of Lincoln (The Great Emancipator has been Invoked by Activists and Idealists of every Stripe, on every Continent)*, by Richard Carwadine. I previously had thought of Lincoln as "ours" because he occupies such a prominent place in U.S. history. He's frequently invoked by presidents, pundits, and political candidates for every office in the land.

I was surprised when I learned about Lincoln's effect on the entire world. As schoolchildren, we all studied his presidency, his role in the war, and his assassination. If we want to learn more, we have thousands of movies and books to choose from. But did you know that his shooting was mourned *worldwide*? Carwadine said that Lincoln's death:

> . . . prompted unprecedented mourning on every continent, among all classes. In the capitals of Europe, grown men wept openly. Spanish progressives, Italian democrats, French republicans, Czech nationalists and others saw him as the enemy of autocratic power and aristocratic privilege. Popular Italian military figure Giuseppe Garibaldi referred to America and Lincoln as "the teacher(s) of liberty to our fathers."

The article described many other examples of Lincoln's influence. For example, in the 1940s, when Kenya began its struggle for independence against the ruling British, Kenyan students used Lincoln's Emancipation Proclamation as a touchstone for their aspirations. In post-World War II Germany—when the country was deeply divided—Willy Brandt, the mayor of Berlin, "apparently found particular value in Lincoln's famous statement, 'a house divided against itself cannot stand.'"

The piece reminded me of the article I wrote about the ECF. Lincoln's influence—his ECF—doesn't diminish. If anything, it expands and comes from unlikely places in every corner of the earth. For example, in 2007 a high-ranking Chinese official cited Lincoln when denouncing Taiwanese and

Tibetan separatism. The Chinese official said, "How come Lincoln's battle to preserve the Union was completely justified, whereas our steadfast effort to maintain a unified motherland is not?" (Those of us who remember the Vietnam War will recall that many in Vietnam considered Ho Chi Ming their Abraham Lincoln.) Whether we agree or disagree with their particular cause, men and women struggling in all manner of circumstances remember and are inspired by the legacy that Lincoln left behind.

Even Lincoln's personal difficulties are considered notable. From what historians have pieced together about his life, Lincoln suffered many bouts of severe depression. He lost two sons while living in the White House and making life-and-death decisions about the war. Yet, one of his most famous lines is: *Most people are about as happy as they make up their minds to be.*

More recently, former U.S. president George Bush used Lincoln to promote an international "freedom agenda." During his eight years in the White House, President Bush ordered that "Lincoln Corners" would be opened in Asian public libraries. These library corners have the expressed purpose of improving U.S. relations with Asia. The Lincoln Corners share information about U.S. business and educational opportunities, U.S. history and culture, and so forth. This was done with the hope of promoting mutual understanding and stronger ties between the two continents.

Given the mission of the Lincoln Corners, it's appropriate that Lincoln was the first U.S. president to correspond with a ruler in Southeast Asia, and that the U.S. Embassy in Kuala Lumpur is named the Lincoln Resource Center.

In 2007, then-Senator Barack Obama announced his candidacy in Springfield, Illinois, in what he described as the "shadow of the Old State Capital, where Lincoln himself had spoken with such eloquence." This site was important to Obama not only because of its symbolic significance, but because Lincoln had also served as a state senator, just as he had. The announcement speech was admired, even by nonsupporters, because the setting unconsciously reminded the country of Lincoln's ECF.

Billions of men and women have lived on our planet, but you and I could probably only name two or three hundred people whose EFC is as enduring, widespread, and inspirational as Lincoln's—Helen Keller, Winston Churchill, Franklin Roosevelt, Eleanor Roosevelt, Martin Luther King, Florence Nightingale, Mohandas Gandhi. There are many religious figures who belong in this elite company, too. As you probably realize, these famous individuals were not necessarily universally loved in their own time. In fact, many lived every day with the knowledge that thousands of people hated them with an intensity that, in some cases, led to violence.

As I was thinking about people with an enduring ECF, Candy Lightner came to mind; she's a person who brought about significant change for the better without arousing much hostility. Of course, she bumped up against certain vested interests. Alcohol producers and bar owners battled the new drinking age and legal blood alcohol limits. MADD had to lobby hard to make its case. As a result, we see stronger enforcement of impaired driving laws—and DUI citations have marred many a public service career. Today, most TV commercials for alcoholic beverages include a message to "drink responsibly." Before MADD, that kind of cautionary message was unheard of.

Not all of us will leave the same kind of ECF as Lincoln and the others, but look at it another way. If you sometimes feel insignificant, consider Lincoln. Pretend for a moment that your actions and words will be remembered and outlive you. The way others remember you is what creates your ECF. What kind of mark do you want to leave behind? If you've been to school, are in the workforce, run your own business, or have relatives and friends, then you've already left your mark on many different people. You have an extensive Emotional Carbon Footprint already.

Have you been leaving good impressions? Are people happy to see you, or do they cringe when they hear your name? What kinds of feelings are evoked when you're mentioned? Asking these questions is a way to start thinking about the big picture of your life. Of course, nobody is perfect, and no one is everybody's cup of tea. Still, we can only control our behavior; the behavior of others is completely irrelevant.

If you want to measure your ECFs—past, present, and future—begin by increasing your self-awareness. Start each day by asking questions and looking within:

> How do I feel today? (Simple question, but not always easy to answer.)
> Am I in touch with my feelings? (This is the path to answering question #1.)
> I want to monitor my behavior, so what effect do my encounters with others have?
> How will people experience me while I'm in my present state of mind?
> Am I taking care of myself, physically as well as mentally?
> Am I smiling?
> What kind of EFC will I leave today?

AN ONGOING PROCESS

After every meeting with someone, take time to examine the experience you had with that person. Then imagine the possibilities of how he or she experienced you. If you regularly look within, soon you'll increase your awareness of the ECFs in your life. Even subtle changes can make your emotional environment much healthier for yourself and others. Self-awareness gives us the ability to unfold and marvel at what makes each person unique and precious. This is what personal growth and change are about. To improve your life, you must enhance the positive effect you have on others.

Since we can't change behaviors and habits that we're unaware of, our most important task is to raise our self-awareness—and that doesn't happen all at once. The best way to do this is through ongoing self-assessment, which helps us identify areas in which we've grown and areas where we can still develop. So, in addition to the questions listed above, I suggest using the queries below to assess where you are and where you want to go on your incredible life journey:

- ✓ With what thoughts do I begin each day?
- ✓ Do I like what I do?
- ✓ Exactly what role do I play in my current life challenges?
- ✓ What behavior prevents me from meeting the kind of people I desire or finding the harmony at work and at home?
- ✓ If I'm not satisfied with my work, social life, or family interactions, what's my part in this dissatisfaction?
- ✓ What do I expect from others?
- ✓ What do I expect from myself?

- ✓ Am I kind to myself and others?
- ✓ Would I mind if my actions were broadcast on the local news program?

As you can see, self-awareness flows into virtually all areas of life. The last question circles back to the concept of ECF by asking us if our public and private behavior are in sync. Would we mind if someone overheard our conversation with a loved one or a coworker? Did our tone match who we want to be? Do our actions reflect who we are?

Remember that our emotions bubble, ripple, and simmer beneath the threshold of awareness. They have a powerful impact on how we perceive and react to all the events of life—be they mundane or profound. Being fully present, taking time to acknowledge your thoughts and emotions, is the first step in your journey of self-awareness.

13

GET A GRIP ON YOUR LIFE

> Follow the 3R's: **R**espect for self, **R**espect for others, and accept **R**esponsibility for all your actions.
> — Dalai Lama

It's time to put together everything that you've learned and move forward with new attitudes and beliefs. It's my hope, of course, that the previous chapters have given you some fresh ideas you can put into action—and there's no time like the present. Perhaps you're motivated to reexamine your assumptions about the world. You've observed your behavior and that of others, finally realizing that *you* are the only person you can control. But isn't that a relief? Just think, others can be friendly one day and scowl at you the next—and you don't need to do a thing about it. You don't even need to "feel" a thing about it.

When I say "a plan for your life," I don't necessarily mean a list, although lists can be helpful. You might not need to change any of your life goals. But if you do choose to let go of excuses and go after what you dream about, don't put on a grim face. You're going about serious business, but you can walk lightly, too. As you develop greater self-awareness—which is the key to achieving a high level of emotional intelligence—you'll find yourself feeling freer to be who you are, which is a sign of the best kind of personal power. That's what getting a grip on your life is all about.

Positive change of any kind requires altering your perception—understanding the way we see things. At any given moment, we're bombarded by more than 2 million bits of sensory stimuli (sight, sound, smell, taste, touch). We note the light beaming across our desk (where did that dust come from?); overhear the buzz of conversation in the next cubicle; catch the aroma of the coffee brewing across the hall; taste the mint we popped in our mouth; and feel the pinch of a tight ring.

But these are only the sensory messages that we're conscious of. Think of what we might be missing—the faint sound of the elevator closing, a faraway copy machine, a quiet radio in the background, the feel of the tweed chair, the scent of furniture polish. We don't necessarily notice the faint tightness in our stomach—a sign of nervousness—or a slight headache that might indicate tension.

Unconsciously, we filter out information that is irrelevant to our needs in the moment. By omitting the unnecessary, we can focus only on what matters to us. At the end of the process—which occurs in a blink of an eye—our perceptions guide our next thought, feeling, or action. In this case, the pain caused by your uncomfortably tight ring wins out over all the other stimuli. Once you're aware of your physical discomfort, the din of conversation recedes. It's as if it isn't there. You twist the ring until you get it off your finger—and then the dust on the desk captures your attention. You ignore it, but now smell of coffee has become more interesting. You walk across the hall and happily fill a mug with freshly brewed coffee. Oh no, here comes Jake, the loudmouth who has always annoyed you. You screw up your face and realize he's seen you. At that point, you don't smell or hear or see anything else. You and Jake are too busy ruining each other's days! You've lost your grip on your life in that moment. However, as you know by now, it doesn't have to be this way.

Getting a grip on my life meant understanding at a deep level that interactions with others truly are an exchange of emotions. Yes, we exchange information through speech—trivial and significant, personal and professional—but emotions are the unseen layer of our interactions that determine the way we feel and the quality of our days. Psychologists have described this emotional quality as the "feeling tone" of an atmosphere or interaction. For example, if we're pleasant and positive, we contribute that feeling tone to the rooms we enter, the meetings we attend, and our family dinners. In one-on-one interactions, we provide 50% of the "feeling tone" of the conversation. On a daily basis, then, we need to ask ourselves about the quality of the 50% we bring to all our interactions.

As we said before, the human brain is hardwired to connect with and mimic the emotions of others. Outside our conscious awareness, a complex network of brain chemicals and hormones guide our own reactions and the reactions of others. This process is *very* complex. In a matter of nanoseconds, we exchange our emotions with one another—reacting, interpreting, feeling, and perhaps acting.

It's a miracle, really, our ability to react and respond in this way, both within and outside of ourselves. But as intricate as this mind-body system is, it's also wonderfully simple. I smile, you smile back; our brain cells send a message that increases our sense of wellbeing—chemicals that lift our moods are elevated. On the other hand, if you cry when we're together, the chemicals in my body change, too, and enable me to feel concern and empathy. I see Jane laughing across the room, and even without the slightest idea what she finds so funny, I might start laughing, too. We should never underestimate the contagious quality of emotions, one-on-one or in a group.

WHERE TO KEEP THE FOCUS

Throughout this book, you've read many examples that illustrate the various ways we can go through life. We can ramble around, figuratively banging into people, stepping on others' toes, creating tension, and hurting feelings—all the while remaining blind to the experience we create for others. We can blame other people for our problems and then spend our time judging. *Tsk, tsk, tsk.* How can our coworkers or families or strangers be so incompetent, unreasonable, or rude? Wouldn't the world be a better place if we were in charge?

Some people never look outside themselves for the source of trouble in their lives. However, most of us eventually get an inkling that something is amiss—or missing. Maybe we're uneasy with our judgmental ways or unhappy that we were passed over for a promotion. A boss may have told us that superior technical skills alone aren't enough. Perhaps we're at odds with family members, maybe seriously so. Somehow we feel that we're falling short of achieving our goals. This uneasy sense—that we're missing important solutions—sends many of us off in search of a different way of looking at life.

Change is hard, and most of us are dragged kicking and screaming before heading in a different, more productive direction. I hope this book will help you to focus during the ups and downs of your life. By increasing your self-awareness and emotional intelligence, you're giving yourself a tremendous gift.

Increased self-awareness improves the quality of your life, moment to moment. You might find that you're better at evaluating the issues within the realm of your control. Perhaps you modulate your behavior and overreact less often.

Goleman and others have pointed out that self-awareness and emotional intelligence can make a big difference in the twists and turns along your career path. Fifty or 100 years ago, the emotional intelligence of a farmer or factory worker didn't mean the difference between success and failure. The field was plowed; the product assembled. However, this kind of emotional neutrality no longer works in the modern world.

Today, we're in the "knowledge-based economy": the next evolution of the "information age," which in turn evolved from "the service economy." More than ever before, workplaces today demand well-developed personality traits. Occupational skills are important, but when we look deeply into what employers desire, we see that they want more. They want to hire, retain, and promote people who have the ability to take responsibility for their actions and work creatively and harmoniously with others. In other words, employers seek self-aware people with a high degree of emotional intelligence. Behind all the interview questions, businesses of all sizes are in search of employees who:

- Know themselves and their emotional "triggers";
- Have the ability to deliver (on promises and obligations in timely, quality manner);
- Are trustworthy (respond to the needs of organizations and other people, not just their own interests);

- Have the ability to access *information, support,* and *resources*;
- Never play power games.

Clearly, when we put these traits together, we see a person who understands emotional intelligence and who exercises their personal power wisely. In short, this is a person with a firm grip on his or her life.

AVOIDING THE PITFALL: ACTIVITY OVERLOAD

We grasp that it's important to understand ourselves and to be intellectually and emotionally skilled. However, before I end this book, I want to examine one pitfall of modern life that is a serious threat to personal power: *activity overload.*

Controlling your life means getting a grip on your time and your schedule. Unfortunately, most of us rush around trying to do too much, with "to-do" lists a mile long. We often set ourselves up to accomplish the impossible, and as a result, our friends and family will accuse us of being impatient, tense, distracted, or forgetful. We have difficulty sleeping, regardless of how tired and worn-out we are. The demands of a heavy schedule can actually chip away at our personal power. When we talk about feeling "drained," or say that a particular person "drains" us, we're using a descriptive word for loss of personal power.

If your days feel frenzied, you have plenty of company. Activity overload is commonly accepted as a normal element of modern life, as if human beings have always lived this way. Activity overload also is one of the primary ways we act against our own self-interest. We cannot develop self-awareness or boost our emotional intelligence if we're pulled in too many directions.

As mentioned earlier, the amygdala in our brain protects us during times of stress and attack. To help us escape from a perceived menace, the amygdala shuts down all nonessential neuro-circuits in the brain. That's why we can't think clearly during activity overload: all of our instincts are focused on survival rather than thinking and reasoning. The more our lives are dominated by activity overload, the more we need to get a grip and take back our personal power.

THE SENSE OF UNFINISHED BUSINESS

Activity overload leads to the constant sense that we're unable to complete our tasks and projects. We might tell other people that we "don't seem to get anything done." We're always speeding along, but never focusing on whatever is happening in the moment. Before we can feel the satisfaction of completing a task, we're on to the next one. Frequently, a demand with greater urgency (or so we think) will yank us away from a not-quite-finished project. Deadlines loom, paper piles up, and next day's schedule gets packed, too.

Why is feeling rushed and "behind" so prevalent today? Certainly, the struggle to balance work and family is an important factor. After being on the job all day, many of us taxi our children around to after-school clubs, sports practice, dance rehearsals, and so on. Don't forget parent-teacher conferences, homework supervision, and activities within our faith communities. We rarely get to see an empty square on the calendar.

Hey, hey! you say, waving your arms at me. Don't forget the grocery shopping and cooking! And then there's laundry and cleaning. Add to this BlackBerrys, cell phones, and email 24/7—the result is a frenzy that saps our creativity, our well-being, and even our essential humanity. After a day that goes on and on, our bodies are ready to stop, but our minds are going full steam ahead, making lists of today's unfinished business and tomorrows demands.

Psychiatrist Dr. Edward Hollowell has come up with a diagnosis for our out-of-control lifestyles: Environmentally Induced Attention Deficit Disorder (EIADD), which he says is caused by activity overload in combination with technology. Our days are so busy with increased speed, stimuli, and numerous demands that many of us end up with a condition similar to Attention Deficit Disorder (ADD)—just like so many of our young people today.

In his book, *Crazy Busy: Overstretched, Overbooked, and about to Snap—Strategies for Coping in a World Gone Mad,* Hollowell contends that feeling overstretched is characteristic of our modern society. We try to do more in less time, but our minds are channel surfing all day long, caught up in how much we have to do. We think about work demands when we're at home and about home demands when we're at work. It even happens during conversations: our bodies might be present, but our minds are elsewhere. Our listening skills suffer in this kind of environment because our minds are always trying to jump ahead to the next thing.

LOSS OF PLEASURE, LOSS OF PERSONAL POWER

A hurried, distracted lifestyle can turn once-pleasurable activities into tremendous burdens. We might enjoy reading to our kids or taking leisurely walks in our neighborhood park, but when we've brought tons of work home from the office, reading a story to our toddler feels like a hassle. We've been robbed! Robbed of pleasure and personal power. As pressures mount, we let go of our hobbies because we don't have time. When we decide we're too busy for the pleasurable things in life—fun or exercise or nurturing ourselves and others—then the quality of our interpersonal relationships go downhill.

Nowadays, it's not unusual to see a couple or a family having dinner in a restaurant, but not really present in an interactive group. Instead, they're lost in their separate worlds of cell phones and texting. It's seems so difficult to just turn these devices off. How often are email messages or phone calls truly urgent? If we're not doctors on call, will it matter if we enjoy a family meal (or finish reading a story to a child) before reading our messages and returning our calls? Almost all of the time, things can wait.

Our frenzied habits can even spill over and harm others. A chaotic environment invites more mistakes and accidents. Industrial safety professionals tell us this all the time. Drivers who see other people texting or talking on the phone behind the wheel tell us the same thing. In this kind of tumultuous atmosphere, otherwise polite people can act rude and unpleasant; those who tend to be happy and receptive become reclusive and disgruntled. What's worse, many people are just unable to take care of themselves. Their focus isn't on others or themselves; it's simply on time pressure, schedules, and demands. Personal power, a sense of autonomy—all of it disappears.

Activity overload prevents us from setting our own tempo, but we can take that power back. Taking charge of our schedules is a sign of emotional intelligence and personal power.

How can we stop the madness and give ourselves the time we need to live sanely, from a place of self-awareness? Hollowell has some suggestions for us:

- **Stop the 24-hour access:** Yes, our families will always have our immediate attention when they need it, but our coworkers, friends, and bosses don't need us when we're in the middle of dinner or riding a bike or reading a book.

- **Schedule time to answer your email, snail mail, and voice mail:** Keep your life separate from the Internet. You're in charge of checking your email. You don't need to check it every few minutes.
- **Turn off the Blackberry and cell phone:** Remember that you're in control of technology. A few decades ago, if we left our house or office, we had no way of knowing if anyone called us. No answering machine, no voice mail—nothing. Just think of how "out of touch" we were! People who really wanted to reach us called back until they caught us at home.
- **Take breaks during the day:** Walk around your office to stretch your legs, or stop at a coworker's desk and have a five-minute friendly conversation. When you go back to work, you'll feel refreshed and ready to focus.
- **Prioritize—in the largest sense of the concept:** Making lists is *not* the same as setting priorities. How often do pleasant activities or breaks turn up on our to-do lists? We might pencil them in our calendars, but the pressure of the day ends up feeling more important. If taking walks in the park or spending quiet time with your children or grandchildren are important activities for you, then you should set boundaries around how late you'll stay at the office or how much work you'll take home. In a larger sense, it could mean rethinking your life. Maybe you'd rather modify your ambitions to allow for the family or personal life you want—and choose.

- A friend of mine turned down two job offers in which management warned that new hires could expect 50–55 hour workweeks. She could've said yes, but that meant significantly altering her life: she'd have to pay for dog sitters to accommodate eleven-hour workdays—plus ninety minutes of commuting. Good grief. As a single woman in her fifties, she wanted a life. If that meant a career change and downsizing her lifestyle, then she realized she was prepared to do it.
- **Establish boundaries with a simple word: No:** You're not obligated to step up every time your family, office, faith community, or volunteer organization comes a'calling. Refusing to say no means that you'll inevitably spread yourself too thin. Sooner or later, you'll find yourself under-performing at all levels. This goes back to priorities. What is most important to you right now?

Healthy boundaries make for a more peaceful, easier flow in life.
– Dr. N. Neill

- **End relationships and withdraw from projects and organizations that drain you:** We have a rule in our house. If we feel worse after spending an evening with someone, we don't go back for more. We simply don't schedule any more evenings with him or her. We really don't have *time* to be emotionally drained by others.
- **Evaluate what you're good at, and do more of it:** Delegate everything else. In other words, play to your strengths and quit trying to become more skilled in your weak areas. Hollowell says that when we do what we're good at, the work can take on the quality of play.
- **Value downtime:** We've all experienced light bulb moments: those magical times when we have a great idea or insight. Some of our best ideas and most creative thoughts come to us when we're taking a hot bath, relaxing on our deck or front porch, or out pulling weeds in the garden. Sometimes we dismiss these precious moments as "downtime." In our society, downtime is considered to be the brief period of rest in between the rushing and chaos, which we spend with our lists in hand. Hallowell tells us that the use of downtime is a forgotten art, and perhaps we'd appreciate it more if we understood its value!
- **Take care of yourself first:** If you're squared away yourself, you'll be available when someone genuinely needs you. As the friendly stewardess on every flight says, "Put your own oxygen mask on first. Then help the person next to you."

- **Finally, Remember WYDIWYG:** *What You Do Is What You Get.*

I keep coming back to this reminder: a simple adage I use to guide my days. What I do is truly what I get, and this awareness has had great implications for my life. It changed my attitude. One day, I realized that when I come home from work and close the door behind me, all I really want is to be at peace. I'm no longer obsessed with measuring how much I accomplish or how many compliments I get. Nor do I chastise myself for small mistakes. I've thrown away my list of petty slights and disagreements. I certainly don't care who bumps into me by accident or who cuts in front of my car.

A state of inner peace and tranquility is infinitely better than constantly running yourself ragged just to please others. This is my focus today. I know that there's nothing wrong with me just because my point of view isn't the same as someone else's. There's a certain contentment in valuing myself. I realize that I have the right to create and maintain boundaries, and that certain thoughts and feelings are mine alone and nobody else's.

This type of serenity isn't developed overnight; it's a process, not an event. There are still days when I struggle to set and maintain my personal boundaries, and it's tough to always keep my composure. But I know that with consistent self-awareness and a sincere commitment to increasing your level of emotional intelligence, you too can take it back—your power that is. I hope this book helps.

> *Control your own destiny or someone else will.* – Jack Welsh

SELECTED BIBLIOGRAPHY

CHAPTER 1

Goleman, Daniel. *Emotional Intelligence*. New York: Bantam Books, 1995.

Marcopolos, Harry. *No One Would Listen: A True Financial Thriller*. Hoboken, NJ: Wiley, 2010.

"The Madoff Affair: Con of the Century." *Economist*, December 20, 2008.

CHAPTER 2

Kreitner, Robert and Angelo Kinicki. *Organizational Behavior*, 9th ed. Boston: Irwin/McGraw-Hill, 2009.

CHAPTER 4

Brinkman, Rick and Rick Kirschner. *Dealing with People You Can't Stand*, 2nd ed. New York: McGraw-Hill, 2002.

Kreitner, Robert and Angelo Kinicki. *Organizational Behavior*, 9th ed. Boston: Irwin/McGraw-Hill, 2009.

Rosenthal, Robert and Lenore Jacobson. *Pygmalion in the Classroom: Teacher Expectation and Pupils' Intellectual Development*. Bancyfelin, Carmarthen, UK: Crown House Publishing, 2003.

CHAPTER 5

Dyer, Wayne. *Excuses Be Gone! How to Change Lifelong, Self-Defeating Thinking Habits*, 4th ed. Carlsbad, CA: Hay House, 2011.

CHAPTER 6

Goleman, Daniel. *Emotional Intelligence*. New York: Bantam Books, 1995.

Kaplan, Bob, Wilfred Drath, and Joan R. Kofodimos. *Beyond Ambition: How Driven Managers Can Lead Better and Live Better*. San Francisco: Jossey-Bass, 1991.

Segal, Jeanne S. *Raising Your Emotional Intelligence*. New York: Holt, 1997.

CHAPTER 7

Brzezinski, Mika. *Knowing Your Value: Women, Money and Getting What You're Worth* New York: Weinstein Books, 2011.

CHAPTER 8

LeDoux, Joseph. *The Emotional Brain: The Mysterious Underpinnings Of Emotional Life*. New York: Simon and Schuster, 1998.

Synaptic Self: *How Our Brains Become Who We Are*, 2nd ed. New York: Penguin, 2003.

CHAPTER 9

Covey, Stephen. *The 7 Habits of Highly Effective People*. New York: Free Press, 1990.

Welstead, Suzanne. *Searching for You: Ideas About Healthy Relationships*. N.p.: Self-published, 2009.

CHAPTER 11

Bernstein, Elizabeth. "I'm Very, Very, Very Sorry . . . Really?" *Wall Street Journal*, October 18, 2010.

CHAPTER 12

Carwadine, Richard. "The Surprising Global Reach of Lincoln," *Wall Street Journal*, May 7, 2011.

CHAPTER 13

Hallowell, Edward. *Crazy Busy: Overstretched, Overbooked, and About to Snap!* New York: Ballantine, 2006.

RECOMMENDED READING

I often mention the following books and articles in my seminars and class lectures. If you'd like to become more familiar with the concepts discussed in this book, you'll find these publications of great help.

Begley, Sharon. *Train Your Mind, Change Your Brain: How a New Science Reveals Our Extraordinary Potential to Transform Ourselves*. New York: Ballantine Books, 2007.

Bolton, Robert and Dorothy Grover Bolton. *People Styles at Work*. New York: AMACOM, 1996.

Boyatzis, Richard and Annie McKee. *Resonant Leadership*. Boston: Harvard Business School Press, 2005.

Boyatzis, Richard, Daniel Goleman, and Annie McKee. *Primal Leadership*. Boston: Harvard Business School Press, 2002.

Gladwell, Malcolm. *The Tipping Point*. Little, Brown and Company, New York 2002.

Goleman, Daniel, *Social Intelligence*. New York: Bantam Books, 2006.

Jones, Gareth and Jennifer George. *Essentials of Contemporary Management*. Boston: McGraw Hill, 2009.

LeDoux, Joseph. "Emotion Circuits in the Brain," *Annual Review of Neuroscience* 23: 155–184.

Pink, Daniel, *A Whole New Mind*. New York: Riverhead Books, 2006.

Schein. Edgar, *Organizational Culture and Leadership*, 4th ed. San Francisco, CA: Jossey-Bass, 2010.

Senge, Peter. *The Fifth Discipline*. New York: Doubleday, 1990.

ABOUT THE AUTHOR

DR. KAY POTETZ is a management consultant and has been conducting seminars since the 1980s. Her qualifications include twenty-five years of management and administrative experience, a Master's Degree in Business Administration, and a Ph.D.

She began her career in hospital work as a licensed Radiological Technologist and moved on to Nuclear Medicine Technology. After many years in health care, she moved from the hospital environment to college teaching.

In addition to coaching and conducting seminars throughout the United States and Canada, Dr. Potetz is an adjunct faculty member at Baldwin Wallace College in Berea, Ohio, and serves as a facilitator for Kent State University's Center for Corporate and Professional Development.

For more information visit *www.DRKKP.com*.